REFLECTIONS ON PROGRESS

Reflections on Progress

ESSAYS ON
THE GLOBAL POLITICAL ECONOMY

KEMAL DERVIŞ

BROOKINGS INSTITUTION PRESS

Washington, D.C.

Copyright © 2016
THE BROOKINGS INSTITUTION
1775 Massachusetts Avenue, N.W., Washington, D.C. 20036
www.brookings.edu

The Brookings Institution is a private nonprofit organization devoted to research, education, and publication on important issues of domestic and foreign policy. Its principal purpose is to bring the highest quality independent research and analysis to bear on current and emerging policy problems. Interpretations or conclusions in Brookings publications should be understood to be solely those of the authors.

Library of Congress Cataloging-in-Publication data are available.

ISBN 978-0-8157-2961-7 (cloth : alk. paper)
ISBN 978-0-8157-2962-4 (ebook)

9 8 7 6 5 4 3 2 1

Typeset in Adobe Jenson Pro

Composition by Elliott Beard

CONTENTS

Part III
EUROPE: BEYOND CRISIS MANAGEMENT 105

PREFACE

A strong belief in continuous human progress has been a legacy of the Enlightenment to many generations. This conviction survived many setbacks, not least those of the first half of the 20th century. The last essay in the second part of this collection argues that, for the first time in decades, the challenges in the economic, political, environmental, and security spheres are shaking humankind's belief in progress. Angry populism and astonishing forms of nihilism are spreading. At the same time, authoritarianism and the cult of the "leader" can be seen gaining momentum in many places, offering a dubious solution to the fear of the future felt by large segments of the world's population.

My conviction in many of these essays is that neither a lack of financial, or natural resources, nor of insufficient technical know-how is slowing potential progress. The binding constraint on progress in this second decade of the 21st century is the ability of nations, various social groups, and citizens to compromise and cooperate. This constraint is embodied in obstacles preventing good governance and reasonable policies, locally, nationally, and globally.

The essays, each first published as my monthly column on the website of Project Syndicate from January 2012 to December 2015, were designed to be timely while dealing with issues of continuing interest in the global political economy. A few columns that had been focused more narrowly on a current event are excluded. The essays broadly fall into three categories: International Economics, Political Economy and Income Distribution, and the Future of Europe. They appear at a time in history when the combination of mind-boggling technological change and the irreversible process of globalization create huge opportunities as well as grave dangers. We have seen transformational technological change in the past, some of it at least as important as what we are experiencing with the digital revolution today, as Roger Gordon again reminded us recently in his excellent book entitled *The Rise and Fall of American Growth*.[1] Nonetheless *the speed of change* in our epoch is of a different order of magnitude and imminent developments in artificial intelligence may eventually become as transformational as electricity or the railroads. Moreover, globalization is more comprehensive and multidimensional than it has ever been, to a large degree again because of the development of communications technologies.

These essays appear in chronological order in each chapter as they were written; the reader can see how the topics and my thinking about them evolved over four years. A few related themes are present in all the essays, often cutting through the categories. Globalization is here to stay, but will it tend to lead the average income levels between nations to converge, or will per capita incomes start to diverge again? Convergence seems to have almost stopped in 2015–16: will this just be a temporary parenthesis, or does it signal a phenomenon that may last?

Another theme relates to the interaction of markets and public policy. National markets have been embedded in national political processes for a long time. The nation-state has regulated, supervised, and redistributed—not always in the best possible way but without doubt adding a much-needed social and regulatory dimension to market economies and contributing to successful societies in the second half of the 20th century. The regulated and socially "softened" market economies with relatively strong social insurance systems triumphed over Soviet-style communism in the 1980s, not the unfettered wild capitalism of the late 19th and early 20th centuries that led to the Great Depression and the rise of totalitarian political systems in reaction to huge inequalities. In the 21st century, something similar to the "institutional embedding" of national markets must happen for global markets to avoid similar catastrophes. While I certainly don't want to fall into the trap of thinking that global government is a feasible or desirable solution, or even that "more government" is what is called for, better governance is today a historical priority. Public policy must be designed and implemented at multiple levels, going from the very local to the national, regional, and global, as emphasized in one of the essays. Governance has to be multilevel and multichannel, involving civil society and private initiative in multifaceted partnerships that cross national borders The important role both cities as well as private business have played in the

December 2015 Climate Summit in Paris, in partnership with national governments, was a good illustration of how issues can and need to be addressed in a multilevel manner. The same partnerships will of course be needed to implement what was no more than an encouraging start.

Moreover, in the 21st century the global dimension of economic "governance" needs to be stronger and more comprehensive than was the system created after World War II. Greater equity and balance in income distribution have become an even bigger issue as new forms of inequality challenge fundamental democratic values as well as socioeconomic stability. The electoral campaign in the United States in 2016 cannot easily be understood without realizing how deeply inequality, real as well as perceived, is disturbing many Americans. Can a society remain democratic in the sense of giving an equal "say" to citizens, when more than 20% of income and about 80% of incremental income go to the top 1%, as has been the case for decades now in the United States?[2] That is increasingly becoming the case in many leading economies, although the electoral process in the United States has also shown that in an advanced country at least, campaigns with a strong message can be financed by small internet-based donations, which compensate to some extent for the weight of very large fortunes.

Economic cross-border spillover effects and economic interdependence have also become more important and need a stronger global framework that can deal with problems such as persistent and large trade imbalances, tax avoidance, and the need to harmonize financial regulation, manage migration, and ensure adequate competition in international markets.

The European Union as a form of "governance beyond the nation-state" is a powerful illustration of both the benefits and the huge difficulties of such cooperation and of multilevel governance in general. If Europe were to fail in creating both vibrant economic progress, equitable distribution, and functioning institutions capable of adapting to the realities of the new century, it would strongly affect the hope for better global governance all over the world. The last four years have been extraordinarily difficult for Europe. The crisis around the Eurozone and Greece in particular, the challenge of achieving closer fiscal and financial policy integration in the Eurozone, while a large number of European Union countries are not in the Eurozone, the fierce debate about austerity, and the huge refugee crisis have shaken the continent to a degree unseen in seven decades. I do believe, even more than before, that the "Two Europes in One" vision constitutes the only way forward, although it will no longer be two Europes in one European Union with the United Kingdom's approval of a referendum to leave the European Union. With two-thirds of the UK's young people voting to stay, however, Brexit should not and will not lead to a full divorce between Europe and the United Kingdom. The essays on Europe in the third part of this volume reflect specifically European issues but are also part of the overall theme of global political economy and better governance.

I would like to thank the Brookings Institution and Strobe Talbott for providing the unique setting in which such essays could be written and Project Syndicate and particularly Ken Murphy for very helpful guidance and edits, as well as many colleagues for their comments, which much improved these essays. Karim Foda has worked with me on related research for most of the time the essays were written. Edith Joachimpillai and Julia Ruiz have also provided invaluable assistance. Jordan Bivings has helped me throughout in putting together this manuscript with great skill and judgment. The final version of this book has much benefited from the careful editing of Janet Walker from the Brookings Institution Press. My wife, Catherine, has always been a tough critic as well as an invaluable and constructive adviser. I owe deep gratitude to all these friends, colleagues, and family.

PART I

GLOBAL ECONOMICS

The concept of a "world" economy dates back to trade taking place over the vast expanses of the Roman Empire or around China under the Han dynasty. It brings up the memory of the ancient Silk Road. With the exchanges and early value-chain integrations that took place under the umbrella of the British Empire in the 19th century, the "world" also became more global.

It is only in the last decade of the 20th century, however, that what I would like to call modern globalization started. A combination of political and technological factors including the collapse of Soviet communism and the development of the internet created a new, more connected and more universal world economy. It is also around 1990 that a new phenomenon of "convergence" took hold: *in the aggregate* the developing and emerging countries started growing, even in per capita terms, substantially faster than the rich advanced economies. The income gap remained wide, but for the first time since the Industrial Revolution the relative gap started to narrow. The "great divergence" that had marked the 19th and most of the 20th centuries seemed to turn into convergence. By the first years of the 21st century, convergence had gathered sufficient scope also to lead to real global economic interdependence: causality now runs both from growth in advanced countries to that in the emerging countries *and* in the other direction. In 1997, when Asia caught the "financial flu," it hardly affected the advanced economies. On the contrary in 2015, when China slowed down, it had a major effect on the world economy as a whole.

The essays in Part I of this collection are concerned with some of the key questions debated in the setting of this new world economy. The first essay relates the issue of global imbalances to that of domestic imbalances linked to income distribution. In both cases the macroeconomic concern arises from an apparent chronic excess of desired savings over desired investment that seems to have plagued the world economy since the great financial crisis of 2008–09. Despite record low interest rates in the major reserve currency economies, desired investment seems to be insufficient to absorb desired savings, something Larry Summers, borrowing a term Alvin Hansen used in the late 1930s, has called "secular stagnation."[3] What are the national versus international dimensions of this problem? What is the role of fiscal policy? How important is the relatively little mentioned, yet huge, current account surplus of northern Europe, which is larger than China's in absolute terms and as a percent of GDP? The secular stagnation hypothesis was introduced by Larry Summers primarily as a "demand-side" problem. Over the years,

Robert Gordon has expressed his doubts about future growth prospects focusing more on the supply side of the economy. He assembled these thoughts in early 2016 in an impressive scholarly book entitled *The Rise and Fall of American Growth*.[4] There is a critical link between the two strands of thought: part of the reason for a low demand for investment in the advanced economies may be due to lower expected returns because of more modest expectations formed in a world where innovations are no longer as transformational as they have been over the last two centuries. That at least is Gordon's thesis, which is not of course shared by the techno-optimists of Silicon Valley. Two essays refer to this debate.

Another group of essays deals with the nature and sustainability of the global per capita income convergence process. Was convergence a three-decade parenthesis in history or will it last? Is it a regional, particularly East Asian process, or a more global one? Will 2015 and 2106, with Brazil's GDP having shrunk by more than 7% and world financial markets periodically panicking about China, have been the beginning of the end of the convergence process or will convergence gather steam again in 2017 and after?

Other essays in this group deal with related specific policy issues of global significance: should trade policy become a tool to combat undesirable exchange rate policies and global imbalances; in other words, should exchange rates become part of a "legal" issue for trade agreements, beyond just being part of the international policy dialogue? Should central banks explicitly target employment as well as inflation? How should one deal with the wide fluctuations in the price of oil? Is there a way to use carbon pricing to achieve a dual objective: reduce greenhouse gas emissions and stabilize energy prices? Finally, two essays address the role of technology in both future economic progress and in new social and regulatory challenges that it creates. Whether technological progress will be able to lift growth prospects again substantially or not, it will be transformational in many ways. Artificial intelligence and bioengineering will bring with it huge challenges for public ethics and regulation.

Different countries may want to deal with new technology in different ways, reflecting different democratic preferences and perhaps even values. Yet, the interdependence of the global economy creates powerful forces for precautionary and regulatory harmonization in many domains. The future of economic progress may well depend more than ever on a new social model that manages to balance incentives for rapid change with the ability to minimize social disruption and ensure a wide access to gains from change.

Part II includes essays exploring in greater depth the need for a new social contract that must reflect all of these developments. The "search" for such a new social contract has been evident in the unusual American electoral campaign of 2016 and is increasingly a mark of political campaigns all over the world.

GLOBAL IMBALANCES AND
DOMESTIC INEQUALITY

Despite years of official talk about addressing global current-account imbalances, they remained one of the world's main economic concerns in 2011. Global imbalances were, to be sure, smaller overall than before the crisis, but they did not disappear. Now some are increasing again, alongside inequality in many countries. That link is no accident.

One often hears calls for global rebalancing whereby emerging-market countries with payments surpluses—China is the most-often mentioned—would stimulate internal demand, so that advanced countries (the largest being the United States) could reduce their deficits and public debts with less threat to their economies' recovery. The net foreign demand created by a reduction in balance-of-payments surpluses abroad would partly offset the weakening of public demand in the U.S. and other high-debt countries as they tightened fiscal policy.

The story should not, however, be just about current-account deficits in advanced countries and surpluses in the emerging countries. Many emerging-market countries—including India, South Africa, Brazil, and Turkey—

actually run current-account deficits. There are also many advanced countries that run a current-account surplus: Germany's has been well publicized since the Eurozone crisis started, but Japan, the Netherlands, Norway, and Sweden run surpluses as well.

So, while global rebalancing does require a reduction of surpluses, the issue is not simply one of shrinking emerging-market surpluses in order to allow a corresponding decline in the deficits of the advanced countries. As we enter 2012, a reduction in Germany's surplus may be more urgent than a reduction in China's, since reducing Germany's surplus will yield more immediate benefits for Europe, where the greatest risks to global recovery lie.

Moreover, the Chinese renminbi is experiencing a fairly steep real appreciation, as inflation in China is rising much more rapidly than in the U.S. or the Eurozone. Indeed, the "German" euro is losing value, despite Germany's large surplus, because it is also the currency of the southern European countries that are in so much trouble.

The Chinese and German current-account surpluses are correctly viewed as an obstacle to recovery, because they subtract from potential world effective demand and contribute to global "planned savings" exceeding "planned investments"—a recipe for recessionary pressure. But the increasing concentration of income and wealth within many countries, foremost the U.S., should attract similar "Keynesian" worries.

An increasing concentration of income and wealth can be viewed as an "internal" imbalance similar in some ways to "external" current-account imbalances, because the highest-earning groups tend to save a much larger share of their income. An ongoing income shift toward the highest earners will tend to lead to higher overall savings, which would have to be compensated by higher investment, higher net exports, or higher public expenditures to avoid recessionary pressure.

While levels of inequality around the world vary widely, the tendency toward greater concentration at the top appears to be a general one, and it is changes in concentration that lead to changes in planned savings. An ongoing trend toward income concentration should be expected to lead to deflationary pressure wherever it takes place.

Of course, other factors, including government policies, can compensate for that pressure. In the U.S., low interest rates and debt-financed consumption by lower-income groups, encouraged by government policy and financial-sector practices, compensated for higher savings at the very top during the precrisis years. Thus, despite record income concentration, the U.S. ran a large current-account deficit. In China, net exports and strong government-supported investment ensured continuous expansion. In Germany, too, net exports increased.

Nonetheless, shifts of income to high-saving groups and increasing current-account surpluses have similar first-round effects on aggregate world savings. Of course, it is only the first-round effects that are similar. Much then depends on whether an increase in a current-account surplus leads to more reserve accumulation or more direct investment abroad; on how different income groups allocate their spending between imports and domestic goods; and on what kind of macroeconomic policies are being pursued.

The full story of imbalances has to include propensities to spend on imports and domestic goods in various countries, as well as the balance between public and private savings. Moreover, it is necessary to complement our concerns about global imbalances with an analysis of how increasing income concentration may be leading to internal imbalances and recessionary pressures that are similar in magnitude.

These imbalances are linked, and both threaten sustainable rapid growth. Global imbalances and rising domestic inequality need to be analyzed and debated together. Only then can they be addressed effectively.

April 23, 2012

A WORLD OF CONVERGENCE

For almost two centuries, starting around 1800, the history of the global economy was broadly one of divergence in average incomes. In relative terms, rich countries got even richer. There was growth in the poorer countries, too, but it was slower than rich-country growth, and the discrepancy in prosperity between rich and poor countries increased.

This divergence was very pronounced in colonial times. It slowed after the 1940s, but it was only around 1990 that an entirely new trend could be observed—convergence between average incomes in the group of rich countries and the rest of the world. From 1990 to 2010, average per capita income in the emerging and developing countries grew almost three times as fast as average income in Europe, North America, and Japan, compared to lower or, at most, equal growth rates for almost two centuries.

This has been a revolutionary change, but will this 20-year-old trend continue? Will convergence remain rapid, or will it be a passing phase in world economic history?

Long-term projections based on short-term trends have often been mistaken. In the late 1950s, after the Soviet Union launched the first spacecraft, eminent Western economists predicted that Soviet income would overtake that of the United States in a few decades. After all, the Soviet Union was investing close to 40% of its GDP, twice the ratio in the West.

Later, in the 1980s, Japan's spectacular growth led some to predict that it would overtake the United States, not only in per capita terms, but even in terms of some measures of economic power.

These kinds of projections have often been based on simple extrapolations of exponential trends. Over two or three decades, substantial differences in compound growth rates quickly generate huge changes in economic size or per capita income.

Will the recent predictions of rapid ongoing global convergence similarly turn out to be wrong, or will most of the emerging countries sustain a large positive growth differential and get much closer to the advanced economies' income levels?

Understanding the phenomenon of "catch-up" growth is key to answering this question. Trade and foreign direct investment have made it much easier for emerging countries to absorb and adapt best-practice technology invented in the advanced economies. The information revolution, allowing much easier access to and diffusion of knowledge, has accelerated the process.

Once they developed the basic institutions needed for a market economy and learned how to avoid serious macroeconomic policy mistakes, emerging countries started benefiting from catch-up growth. Those with very high investment rates, mostly in East Asia, grew faster than those with lower investment rates; but, overall, catch-up growth probably has been adding 2 to 4 percentage points to many emerging and developing countries' annual growth rates. At the same time, population growth decreased, adding at least another point to the pace of per capita growth.

This process will likely continue for another decade or two, depending on where in the process particular countries are. It is true that catch-up growth is easier in manufacturing than in other sectors, a point recently emphasized by Dani Rodrik of Harvard University, and it may be that a good portion of it has been exhausted in manufacturing by the best-performing firms in emerging countries.

But there is still a lot of "internal" room for catch-up growth, as less efficient domestic firms become more competitive with more efficient ones. The dispersion of "total factor productivity"—the joint productivity of capital and labor—inside emerging countries has been found to be large. Moreover, sectors such as agriculture, energy, transport, and trade also have catch-up-growth potential, through imports of technology, institutional know-how, and organizational models.

Of course, temporary disturbances, a worsening of

global payments imbalances, or macroeconomic policy mistakes, including those made in advanced economies and affecting the entire world economy, could undermine global growth. But the underlying "convergence differential," owing to catch-up growth, is likely to continue to reduce the income gap between the old advanced economies and emerging-market countries.

The Soviet Union never was able to build the institutions to allow for catch-up economic growth. Japan slowed down after it had basically caught up. China, India, Brazil, Turkey, and others may have firms operating close to the world's technological frontier, but they still have a lot of unused catch-up potential.

The more that these countries can invest while ensuring macroeconomic stability and balance-of-payments sustainability, the faster they can adopt better technology and production processes. In that case, they can continue to catch up, at least for the next decade or more. The convergence process is going to slow, but not yet.

June 8, 2012

AUSTERE GROWTH?

The German government's reaction to newly elected French President François Hollande's call for more growth-oriented policies was to say that there should be no change in the Eurozone's austerity programs. Rather, growth-supporting measures, such as more lending by the European Investment

Bank or issuing jointly guaranteed project bonds to finance specific investments, could be "added" to these programs.

Many inside and outside Germany declare that both austerity and more growth are needed, and that more emphasis on growth does not mean any decrease in austerity. The drama of the ongoing Eurozone crisis has focused attention on Europe, but how the austerity-growth debate plays out there is more broadly relevant, including for the United States.

Three essential points need to be established. First, in a situation of widespread unemployment and excess capacity, short-run output is determined primarily by demand, not supply. In the Eurozone's member countries, only fiscal policy is possible at the national level, because the European Central Bank (ECB) controls monetary policy. So, yes, more immediate growth does require slower reduction in fiscal deficits.

The only counterargument is that slower fiscal adjustment would further reduce confidence and thereby defeat the purpose by resulting in lower private spending. This might be true if a country were to declare that it was basically giving up on fiscal consolidation plans and the international support associated with it, but it is highly unlikely if a country decides to lengthen the period of fiscal adjustment in consultation with supporting institutions such as the International Monetary Fund. Indeed, the IMF explicitly recommended slower fiscal consolidation for Spain in its 2012 *World Economic Outlook*.[5]

Without greater short-term support for effective demand, many countries in crisis could face a downward spiral of spending cuts, reduced output, higher unemployment, and even greater deficits, owing to an increase in safety-net expenditures and a decline in tax revenues associated with falling output and employment.

Second, it is possible, though not easy, to choose fiscal-consolidation packages that are more growth friendly than others. There is the obvious distinction between investment spending and current expenditure, which Italian Prime Minister Mario Monti has emphasized. The former, if well designed, can lay the foundations for longer-term growth.

There is also the distinction between government spending with high multiplier effects, such as support to lower-income groups with a high propensity to spend, and tax reductions for the rich, a substantial portion of which would likely be saved.

Last but not least, there are longer-term structural reforms, such as labor-market reforms that increase flexibility without leading to large-scale lay-offs (a model rather successfully implemented by Germany). Similarly, retirement and pension reforms can increase long-term fiscal sustainability without generating social conflict. A healthy older person may well appreciate part-time work if it comes with flexibility. The task is to integrate such work into the overall functioning of the labor market with the help of appropriate regulation and incentives.

Finally, particularly in Europe, where countries are closely linked by trade, a coordinated strategy that allows more time for fiscal consolidation and formulates growth-friendly policies would yield substantial benefits compared to individual countries' strategies, owing to positive spillovers (and avoidance of stigmatization of particular countries). There should be a European growth strategy, rather than Spanish, Italian, or Irish strategies. Countries like Germany that are running a current-account surplus would also help themselves by helping to stimulate the European economy as a whole.

Slower fiscal retrenchment, space for investment in government budgets, growth-friendly fiscal packages, and coordination of national policies with critical contributions from surplus countries can go a long way in helping Europe to overcome its crisis in the medium term. Unfortunately, Greece has become a special case, one that requires focused and specific treatment, most probably involving another round of public-debt forgiveness.

But insufficient and sometimes counterproductive actions, coupled with panic and overreaction in financial markets, have brought some countries, such as Spain, which is a fundamentally solvent and strong economy, to the edge of the precipice, and with it the whole Eurozone. In the immediate short run, nothing makes sense, not even a perfectly good public-investment project, or recapitalization of a bank, if the government has to borrow at interest rates of 6% or more to finance it.

These interest rates must be brought down through ECB purchases of government bonds on the secondary market until low-enough announced target levels for borrowing costs are reached, and/or by the use of European Stability Mechanism resources. The best solution would be to reinforce the effectiveness of both channels by using both—and by doing so immediately.

Such an approach would provide the breathing space needed to restore confidence and implement reforms in an atmosphere of moderate optimism rather than despair. The risk of inaction or inappropriate action has reached enormous proportions.

No catastrophic earthquake or tsunami has destroyed southern Europe's productive capacity. What we are witnessing—and what is now affecting the whole world—is a man-made disaster that can be stopped and reversed by a coordinated policy response.

December 19, 2012

SHOULD CENTRAL BANKS TARGET EMPLOYMENT?

On December 12, U.S. Federal Reserve Chairman Ben Bernanke announced that the Fed will keep interest rates at close to zero until the unemployment rate falls to 6.5%, provided inflation expectations remain subdued. While the Fed's governing statutes, unlike those of the European Central Bank, explicitly include a mandate to support employment, the announcement marked the first time that the Fed tied its interest-rate policy to a numerical employment target. It is a welcome breakthrough, and one that should be emulated by others—not least the ECB.

Central banks' statutes differ in terms of the objectives that they set for monetary policy. All include price stability. Many add a reference to general economic conditions, including growth and employment or financial stability. Some give the central bank the authority to set an inflation target unilaterally; others stipulate coordination with the government in setting the target.

There is no recent example, however, of a major central bank setting a numerical employment target. This should change, as the size of the employment challenge facing the advanced economies becomes more apparent. Weak labor markets, low inflation, and debt overhang suggest that a fundamental reordering of priorities is in order. In Japan, Shinzo Abe, the incoming prime minister, is signaling the same set of concerns, although he seems to be proposing a "minimum" inflation target for the Bank of Japan, rather than a link to growth or employment.

The spread of global value-chains that integrate hundreds of millions of developing-country workers into the global economy, as well as new labor-saving technologies, imply little chance of cost-push wage inflation. Likewise, the market for long-term bonds indicates extremely low inflation expectations (of course, interest rates are higher in cases of perceived sovereign default or re-denomination risk, such as in southern Europe, but that has nothing to do with inflation). Moreover, the deleveraging under way since the 2008 financial implosion could be easier if inflation were moderately higher for a few years, a debate the International Monetary Fund encouraged a year ago.

Together with these considerations, policymakers should take into account the tremendous human and economic costs of high unemployment, ranging from the millions of shattered lives, skills erosion, and disappearance of opportunities for an entire generation, to the deadweight loss of idle human resources. Is the failure to ensure that millions of young people acquire the skills required to participate in the economy not as great a liability for a society as a large stock of public debt?

Nowhere is this reordering of priorities more needed than in the Eurozone. Yet, strangely, it is the Fed, not the ECB, that has set an unemployment target. The U.S. unemployment rate has declined to around 7.7% and the current-account deficit is close to $500 billion, while Eurozone unemployment is at a record high, near 12%, and the current account shows a surplus approaching $100 billion.[6]

If the ECB's inflation target were 3%, rather than close to but below 2%, and Germany, with the world's largest current-account surplus, encouraged 6% wage growth and tolerated 4% inflation—implying modest real-wage growth in excess of expected productivity gains—the Eurozone adjustment process would become less politically and economically costly. Indeed, the policy calculus in northern Europe greatly underestimates the economic losses due to the disruptions imposed on the south by excessive austerity and wage deflation. The resulting high levels of youth unemployment, health problems, and idle production capacity also all have a substantial impact on demand for imports from the north.

Contrary to conventional wisdom, the ECB's legal mandate would allow such a reordering of priorities, as, with reference to the ECB, the Treaty on the Functioning of the European Union states, "The *primary* [emphasis added] objective of the European System of Central Banks . . . shall be to maintain price stability," and there is another part of the treaty dealing with general Eurozone economic policies that emphasizes employment. This would seem not to preclude a temporary complementary employment objective for the ECB at a time of exceptional challenge.[7]

Moreover, the ECB has the authority to set the Eurozone-wide inflation target and could set it higher for two or three years, without any treaty violation. The real problem is the current political attitude in Germany. Somehow, the memory of hyperinflation in the early 1920s seems scarier than that of massive unemployment in the early 1930s, although it was the latter that fueled the rise of Nazism. Maybe the upcoming German elections will allow progressive forces to clarify what is at stake for Germany and Europe—indeed, the entire world.

In a more global context, none of this is to dismiss the longer-term dangers of inflation. In most countries, at most times, inflation should be kept very low—and central banks should anchor inflation expectations with a stable long-term target, although the alternative of targeting nominal GDP deserves to be discussed.[8]

Moreover, monetary policy cannot be a long-term substitute for structural reforms and sustainable budgets. Long periods of zero real interest rates carry the danger of asset bubbles, misallocation of resources, and unintended effects on income inequality, as recent history—not least in the United States and Japan—demonstrates.

For the coming two to three years, however, particularly in Europe, the need for deleveraging, the costs of widespread joblessness, and the risk of social collapse make the kind of temporary unemployment target announced by the Fed highly desirable.

March 11, 2013

THE GREAT DISCONNECT

Since the second half of 2012, financial markets have recovered strongly worldwide. Indeed, in the United States, the Dow-Jones industrial average reached an all-time high in early March, having risen by close to 9% since September. In Europe, European Central Bank President Mario Draghi's "guns of August" turned out to be remarkably effective.[9] Draghi reversed the euro's slide into oblivion by promising potentially unlimited purchases of member governments' bonds. Between September 1 and February 22, the FTSEurofirst index rose by almost 7%. In Asia, too, financial markets are up since September, most dramatically in Japan.

Even the Italian elections in late February seem not to have upset markets too much (at least so far). Although interest-rate spreads for Italian and Spanish ten-year bonds relative to German bonds briefly jumped 30–50 basis points after the results were announced,[10] they then eased to 300–350 basis points, compared to 500–600 basis points before the ECB's decision to establish its "outright monetary transactions" program.

But this financial market buoyancy is at odds with political events and real economic indicators. In the United States, economic performance improved only marginally in 2012, with annual GDP rising by 2.3%, up from 1.8% in 2011.[11] Unemployment remained high, at 7.8% at the end of 2012, and there has been almost no real wage growth over the last few years.[12] Median household income in the

United States is still below its 2007 level—indeed, close to its level two decades ago—and roughly 90% of all U.S. income gains in the postcrisis period have accrued to the top 1% of households.[13]

Indicators for the Eurozone are even worse. The economy contracted in 2012, and wages declined, despite increases in Germany and some northern countries. Reliable statistics are not yet available, but poverty in Europe's south is increasing for the first time in decades.

On the political front, the United States faces a near-complete legislative stalemate, with no sign of a compromise that could lead to the optimal policy mix: short-term support to boost effective demand and long-term structural reforms and fiscal consolidation. In Europe, Greece has been able—so far—to maintain a parliamentary majority in support of the coalition government, but there, and elsewhere, hyper-populist parties are gaining ground.

The Italian election results could be a bellwether for Europe. Beppe Grillo's populist Five Star Movement emerged with 25% of the popular vote—the highest support for any single party. Former Prime Minister Silvio Berlusconi, confounding those who had forecast his political demise, reemerged at the head of a populist-rightist coalition that ended up only 0.3 percentage points away from winning.

In short, we are witnessing a rapid decoupling between financial markets and inclusive social and economic well-being. In the U.S. and many other places, corporate profits as a share of national income are at a decades-long high, in part owing to labor-saving technology in a multitude of sectors. Moreover, large corporations are able to take full advantage of globalization (for example, by arbitraging tax regimes to minimize their payments).

As a result, the income of the global elite is growing both rapidly and independently of what is happening in terms of overall output and employment growth. Demand for luxury goods is booming, alongside weak demand for goods and services consumed by lower-income groups.

All of this is happening in the midst of extremely expansionary monetary policies and near-zero interest rates, except in the countries facing immediate crisis. Structural concentration of incomes at the top is combining with easy money and a chase for yield, driving equity prices upward.

And yet, despite widespread concern and anxiety about poverty, unemployment, inequality, and extreme concentration of incomes and wealth, no alternative growth model has emerged. The opposition to the dominant mainstream in Europe is split between what is still too often an "old" left that has trouble adjusting to 21st-century realities, and populist, anti-foreigner, and sometimes outright fascist parties on the right.

In the United States, the far right shares many of the characteristics of its populist European counterparts. But it is a tribute to the American two-party system's capacity for political integration that extremist forces remain marginalized, despite the rhetoric of the Tea Party. President Barack Obama, in particular, has been able to attract support as a liberal-left idealist and as a centrist-realist at the same time, which enabled him to win reelection in the face of a weak economy and an even weaker labor market.

Nonetheless, without deep socioeconomic reforms, America's GDP growth is likely to be slow at best, while its political system seems paralyzed. Nowhere is there a credible plan to limit the concentration of wealth and power, broaden economic gains through strong real-income growth for the poor, and maintain macroeconomic stability.

The absence of such a plan in the United States (and in Europe) has contributed to the decoupling of financial markets from inclusive economic progress, suggesting that current trends are politically sustainable. But, while this disconnect could continue for some time if no alternative program emerges, the huge gap between financial markets' performance and most people's well-being is unlikely to persist in the longer term. When asset prices overshoot reality, eventually they have nowhere to go but down.

October 3, 2013

THE END OF CONVERGENCE?

Until recently, there was a broad consensus that this was to be the emerging countries' century. But financial markets' reaction to the U.S. Federal Reserve's warning in May that it may wind down its unconventional monetary policies led many analysts to question how rapid emerging-market growth would be. At this month's Annual Meetings of the World Bank Group and the International Monetary Fund, the emerging countries' prospects will be a topic of heated debate.

Until mid-2013, the IMF and the World Bank had projected aggregate per capita GDP growth rates for the emerging and developing countries (EMDEVs) to be almost 3 percentage points higher than in the world's advanced countries over the next few years. Most commentators expected a substantial difference in per capita growth to continue beyond this decade, disagreeing only about the magnitude of the emerging countries' growth advantage.

Arvind Subramanian's estimates for China, and Uri Dadush's for EMDEVs more generally, represented the upper range of these projections.[14] Others, such as Dani Rodrik, have always been more cautious, arguing that much of the past rapid growth in major EMDEVs was due to a period of technological "catch-up" growth in manufacturing, which was reaching its limits and could not be easily extended to the large service sector or other parts of developing economies.[15]

As it turned out, a mini-crisis followed Federal Reserve Board Chairman Ben Bernanke's announcement that the Fed might "taper" its quantitative-easing (QE) policy—its open-ended commitment to monthly purchases of long-term assets worth $85 billion—before the end of 2013. Many emerging economies' stock markets and currencies took a large hit, and headlines were soon announcing the end of the emerging-market boom.

To be sure, many emerging-market asset values have recovered ground since, and in September the Fed changed its mind about the imminence of tapering QE. But the mood had changed, and the *median* projection of emerging economies' growth prospects has shifted. Latin American economists are particularly pessimistic. After revising downward in July its growth projections for emerging countries, the IMF is about to do so again (though only moderately) ahead of the Annual Meetings.

Do recent events mean that convergence is ending? Is the world reverting to a growth pattern whereby the percentage gap between income levels in the aggregate "North" and "South" does not decrease? Or is the current talk about the "end of convergence" merely a reflection of financial markets' usual overreaction to both good and bad news?

The future, of course, is uncertain. But I continue to believe that convergence is here to stay, though it will not occur at the extraordinary pace of the 2008–12 period, when the global financial crisis and the Eurozone's difficulties led to particularly slow growth in the advanced economies.[16] What is likely is a return to the precrisis differential: from 1990 to 2008 (excluding the 1997–98 Asian financial crisis), aggregate per capita growth in the emerging world was about 2.5 percentage points higher than that in the advanced countries. In the 2008–12 period, that differential increased to more than 4 percentage points. It now appears set to fall back to about 2.5 percentage points.

China will continue to account for a big part of the differential. While China's annual growth may decline to 6%–7%, from the 9%–10% rate recorded until 2010, China's economic weight is increasing. Moreover, emerging Asia as a whole has remained on a convergence path, as have countries like Turkey, Colombia, Peru, and Chile. Technological catch-up will remain the underlying driver of convergence, beyond the short-term shocks and temporary problems that capital-flow volatility may cause.

Of course, "prudent" countries, with small current-account deficits or surpluses, will be much more immune to temporary shocks. Diversified economies will also tend to do better relative to primary-goods exporters. Moreover, countries that invest 25% or more of their national income will be able to grow faster than those—including many in Latin America—with low levels of savings and investment. Asia will grow faster because it is accumulating physical and human capital more rapidly, which not only increases output directly, but also facilitates technological progress and diversification of the type that Ricardo Hausmann and Cesar Hidalgo identify as the key to sustained growth.[17]

Convergence has never taken hold for all EMDEVs; but it has already changed the nature and structure of the world economy, particularly in terms of the traditional north-south divide, and it will continue to do so. Aggregate growth trends have decoupled, though cycles within these trends are correlated, owing to financial globalization and trade interdependencies. A serious slowdown in emerging economies would lead to another marked slowdown in the advanced economies, too, so that the growth differential would likely remain relatively stable, at least in yearly data.

Long-term growth is determined by the ability to accumulate technological and institutional capacities and the quality of national policies. Over the last two decades, many emerging countries, including some of the largest, have performed well in this respect. Their efforts will remain the basis for aggregate convergence. We should not allow the many exceptions or temporary financial-market worries to obscure this underlying reality.

November 22, 2013

NORTHERN EUROPE'S DRAG ON
THE WORLD ECONOMY

In recent years, China's current-account surpluses—which have averaged almost $220 billion annually since 2000—have attracted much criticism from the rest of the world. But Germany's similar-size surpluses—which have averaged about $170 billion since the euro's introduction in 1999—have, until recently, largely escaped scrutiny.

The difference, it was argued, was monetary union. So long as the Eurozone as a whole was relatively balanced, Germany's surpluses were considered irrelevant—just as, say, Texas's surpluses have never been considered an issue in the United States. Chinese surpluses, by contrast, were seen as a cause of global imbalances.

This argument is correct in the sense that it is the current-account surplus or deficit of a monetary union as a whole that can be expected to have exchange-rate implications. And, unlike China, Germany no longer has a "national" exchange rate that can adjust in response to its current-account surplus. These factors—together with the lack of trade data for regions within countries—have led economists only rarely to consider countries' internal surpluses or deficits.

But, in net terms, a region within a country—or, like Germany, a country or subregion within a monetary union—still "subtracts" from national and global aggregate demand if it exports more than it imports. Witness how expenditure cuts by U.S. state governments—many of which are constitutionally required to balance their budgets—frustrated, to some degree, America's massive federal-government stimulus in 2010–11.

For this reason, it is relevant to ask whether a country as large as Germany—or even a large state like California or Texas—augments or depletes global aggregate demand. (In fact, as sovereign countries, California and Texas would have been the world's 12th and 14th largest economies, respectively, in 2012—ahead of the Netherlands, Mexico, and South Korea.)

That question is all the more important, because the Netherlands and Austria, two of Germany's northern European Eurozone neighbors, continue to run current-account surpluses, while the southern European crisis countries have reversed their previously large deficits, as austerity has squeezed domestic demand and made room for an increase in exports. As a result, the Eurozone as a whole will produce a surplus close to $260 billion this year, which represents a new global imbalance that is more directly comparable to China's in the past decade.

Europe's non-Eurozone surplus countries—Sweden, Denmark, Switzerland, and Norway (all of which tie their exchange rates to the euro to some degree)—magnify this global imbalance. Northern Europe—including these four countries and Germany, the Netherlands, and Austria—is running a massive current-account surplus of about $550 billion. Meanwhile, China's surplus is unlikely to exceed $150 billion this year. In fact, the highest level that China's annual surplus has ever reached was around $400 billion in 2007–08—when the United States was poised to introduce trade sanctions against the country, because it viewed this imbalance as a threat to the stability of the U.S. and the world economy.

What is most problematic about the Eurozone's situation is that unemployment in some of the crisis countries—Spain and Greece—remains above 20%. These countries are trying to achieve a difficult "internal devaluation"—that is, a reduction in their domestic unit labor costs relative to the Eurozone's stronger economies—while the overall Eurozone surplus caused by Northern Europe puts upward pressure on the exchange rate, undermining their competitiveness outside the monetary union.

Spain and Greece have managed to achieve an internal devaluation of about 5% this year vis-à-vis Germany, but their competitiveness vis-à-vis the United States and dollar-linked countries has not improved, because the euro has appreciated by more than 5% against the dollar. And, indeed, the euro should appreciate, because the Eurozone as a whole is now running a large current-account surplus.

One can only pity the southern European countries. They should almost thank the French for their inability to impose effective austerity measures and thereby still run a small current-account deficit, which has prevented the Eurozone surplus from becoming even larger.

But an abundance of pity alone will not help. Northern European countries, which have ample room to increase wages and implement expansionary policies, must do so. This would directly benefit northern European citizens themselves, while helping to keep the euro down and stimulate growth and adjustment in southern Europe and the global economy as a whole.

December 17, 2013

CATCHING UP AT DIFFERENT SPEEDS

With weak demand in advanced countries now impeding growth in emerging economies, including major players in Asia and Latin America, many are arguing that the era of income convergence has come to an end. Nothing could be further from the truth.

As I have argued before, convergence of emerging countries' real average incomes, in the aggregate, with advanced countries' incomes is likely to continue into the 2020s. That process started in the late 1980s, and continued unabated, except in the years around the Asian financial crisis in 1997–98. The pace of convergence accelerated further during, and just after, the global financial crisis of 2008–09: the aggregate average differential in per capita income growth increased to more than 4 percentage points in the 2008–12 period, from a little more than 2 percentage points in the two decades before. As the advanced economies recover, however weakly, the growth differential is likely to narrow again, perhaps to about 2 percentage points, which still implies steady convergence at a decent pace.

In that sense, it is not the "end of the party" for emerging markets, as some claimed early last summer, when U.S. Federal Reserve Chairman Ben Bernanke's suggestion of a possible "taper" of the Fed's policy of quantitative easing triggered a mini-crisis in several of the more vulnerable emerging markets.[18] These economies have since recovered a significant part of the lost ground in terms of exchange rates and asset prices.

A major part of the economic-convergence process that has been taking place since the late 1980s has been due to catch-up growth. The emerging markets developed the institutions and the skills base needed to import and adapt technology, which is easier than generating new technology from scratch. The pace of catch-up growth declines only gradually over time, as the less advanced economies slowly move closer to the technological frontier.

The catch-up process also takes place within countries, as labor moves from low-productivity rural activities to higher-productivity urban activities, and as low-productivity firms in all sectors emulate their more advanced domestic counterparts. Moreover, the transfer and diffusion of technology has been facilitated greatly over the last few decades by increased foreign direct investment, the information revolution (which has facilitated access to knowledge), increased trade, and the globalization of financial markets.

These factors apply to emerging countries generally. Why, then, do Latin American economists seem to share a cautious—even pessimistic—mood about future growth and convergence in the region, whereas most Asian economists, while conceding that further structural reforms are needed, believe strongly that Asia will continue to converge rather rapidly?

Beyond global factors that apply to all, rapid catch-up growth requires sufficient investment in both physical and human capital. New manufacturing techniques and new products or product improvements are usually embodied in new machines and skills. China has invested about 43% of its GDP, on average, during the 2000–13 period.

Emerging Asia, excluding China but including India, has invested about 28% of GDP over the same period, while the investment share for Latin America has been just 21%. That alone probably explains much of the difference among China, in a category of its own, emerging Asia, and Latin America. The quality of skills and education cannot be measured as easily by a single figure, but ample evidence shows that Latin America has also lagged behind most of Asia when it comes to skills accumulation.[19]

Many other factors, of course, influence growth and convergence: macroeconomic stability, the efficiency and robustness of the financial sector, the terms of trade, the quality of public administration, demographic factors, and political factors. There also is variation within regions, including among provinces of China. (Likewise, Africa's growth performance has improved spectacularly since the turn of the century, but variance within the continent is even larger than elsewhere.) Nonetheless, in terms of the likely strength of the convergence process that globalization has facilitated, it is important to distinguish between Latin America and Asia, and, within Asia, to distinguish China from the rest of the continent.

China's economy will most likely continue to converge rapidly, though its annual growth rate may fall from 9% to 7%. The rest of emerging Asia will also converge reasonably quickly, though not as quickly as China. Latin America, however, will likely converge only very slowly in the absence of major structural reforms that increase its ability to invest and improve the quality of education.

There will surely be exceptions to this general trend, but there are some stable regional characteristics. Overall, however, basic economics, which has always stressed the need to save and invest in order to grow, still explains a lot. Latin America and Asia operate in the same global economy, with access to similar technology and markets. If Latin America invests around 20% of its national income in a sustained manner, while emerging Asia invests close to 30%—including investments in education—emerging Asia will converge significantly more rapidly.

February 17, 2014

TAILSPIN OR TURBULENCE?

Since the beginning of the year, a new wave of doubt has engulfed emerging markets, driving down their asset prices. The initial wave struck in the spring of 2013, following the Federal Reserve's announcement that it would begin "tapering" its monthly purchases of long-term assets, better known as quantitative easing (QE). Now that the taper has arrived, the emerging-market bears are ascendant once again.[20]

Pressure has been strongest on the so-called Fragile Five: Brazil, India, Indonesia, South Africa, and Turkey (not counting Argentina, where January's mini-crisis started). But worries have extended to other emerging economies, too. Will the Fed's gradual reduction of QE bring with it more emerging-market problems this year? To what extent are today's conditions comparable to those that triggered the Asian crisis of 1997 or other abrupt capital-flow reversals in recent decades?

Emerging-market bulls point out that most major middle-income countries have substantially lowered their public debt/GDP ratios, giving them fiscal space that they lacked in the past. But neither the Mexican Tequila crisis of 1994 nor the Asian crisis of 1997 was caused by large public deficits. In both cases, the effort to defend a fixed exchange rate in the face of capital-flow reversals was a major factor, as was true in Turkey in the year prior to its currency collapse in February 2001.

Today, most emerging countries not only have low public-debt burdens, but also seem committed to flexible exchange rates and appear to have well-capitalized banks, regulated to limit foreign-exchange exposure. Why, then, has there been so much vulnerability?

To be sure, the weakest-looking emerging countries have large current-account deficits and low net central bank reserves after deducting short-term debt from gross reserves. But one could argue that if there is a capital-flow reversal, the exchange rate would depreciate, causing exports of goods and services to increase and imports to decline; the resulting current-account adjustment would quickly reduce the need for capital inflows. Given fiscal space and solid banks, a new equilibrium would quickly be established.

Unfortunately, the real vulnerability of some countries is rooted in private-sector balance sheets, with high leverage accumulating in both the household sector and among nonfinancial firms. Moreover, in many cases, the corporate sector, having grown accustomed to taking advantage of cheap funds from abroad to finance domestic activities, has significant foreign-currency exposure.

Where that is the case, steep currency depreciation would bring with it serious balance-sheet problems, which, if large enough, would undermine the banking sector, despite strong capital cushions. Banking-sector problems would, in turn, require state intervention, causing the public-debt burden to rise. In an extreme case, a "Spanish" scenario could unfold (though without the constraint of a fixed exchange rate, as in the Eurozone).

It is this danger that sets a practical and political limit to flexible exchange rates. Some depreciation can be managed by most of the deficit countries; but a vicious circle could be triggered if the domestic currency loses too much value too quickly. Private-sector balance-sheet problems would weaken the financial sector, and the resulting pressure on public finances would compel austerity, thereby constraining consumer demand—and causing further damage to firms' balance sheets.

To prevent such a crisis, therefore, the exchange rate has to be managed—and in a manner that depends on a country's specific circumstances. Large net central bank reserves can help ease the process. Otherwise, a significant rise in interest rates must be used to retain short-term capital and allow more gradual real-sector adjustment. Higher interest rates will of course lead to slower growth and lower employment, but such costs are likely to be smaller than those of a full-blown crisis.

The challenge is more difficult for countries with very large current-account deficits. And it becomes harder still if political turmoil or tension is thrown into the mix, as has been the case recently in a surprisingly large number of countries.

Nonetheless, despite serious dangers for a few countries, an overall emerging-market crisis is unlikely in 2014. Actual capital-flow reversals have been very limited, and no advanced country will raise interest rates sharply; in fact, with the United States' current-account deficit diminishing, net flows from the U.S. have increased over the last 12 months.[21]

Moreover, most emerging-market countries have strong enough fiscal positions and can afford flexible enough exchange rates to manage a nondisruptive adjustment to moderately higher global interest rates. Much of the recent turmoil reflects the growing realization that financial-asset prices worldwide have been inflated by extraordinarily expansionary monetary policies. As a result, many financial assets have become vulnerable to even minor shifts in sentiment, and this will continue until real interest rates approach more "normal" long-run levels.

In the medium term, however, the potential for technological catch-up growth and secular convergence remains strong in most emerging countries. The pace of a country's convergence will depend, even more than in the past, on the quality of governance and the pace of structural reforms.

April 15, 2014

THE FUTURE OF ECONOMIC PROGRESS

Slowly but surely, the debate about the nature of economic growth is entering a new phase. The emerging questions are sufficiently different from those of recent decades that one can sense a shift in the conceptual framework that will structure the discussion of economic progress—and economic policy—from now on.

The first question, concerning the potential pace of future economic growth, has given rise to serious disagreement among economists. Robert Gordon of Northwestern University, for example, believes that the U.S. economy will be lucky to achieve 0.5% annual per capita growth in the medium term. Others, perhaps most carefully Dani Rodrik, have developed a version of growth pessimism for the emerging economies.[22] The key premise, common to many of these leading analysts, is that technological progress will slow, including the catch-up gains that are most relevant for emerging and developing countries.

On the opposite side are the "new technologists."[23] They argue that we are at the beginning of a fourth industrial revolution, characterized by truly "intelligent machines" that will become almost perfect substitutes for low- and medium-skill labor. These "robots" (some in the form of software), as well as the "Internet of things," will usher in huge new productivity increases in areas such as energy efficiency, transport (for example, self-driving vehicles), medical care, and customization of mass production, thanks to 3D printing.

Second, there is the question of income distribution. In his instantly famous book, Thomas Piketty argues that fundamental economic forces are fueling a persistent rise in profits as a share of total income, with the rate of return on capital constantly higher than the rate of economic growth.[24] Moreover, many have observed that if capital is becoming a close substitute for all but very highly skilled labor, while education systems need long adjustment times to supply the new skills in large quantities, much greater wage differentials between highly skilled and all other labor will cause inequality to worsen.

Perhaps the U.S. economy in ten years will be one in which the top 5%—large capital owners, very highly skilled wage earners, and global winner-take-all performers—get 50% of national income (the percentage is not far below 40% today). Though national circumstances still differ greatly, the fundamental economic trends are global. Are they politically sustainable?

The third question concerns the employment effects of further automation. As was true in previous industrial revolutions, human beings may be freed from much "tedious" work. There will be no need for cashiers, call operators, and toll collectors, for example, and less need for accountants, travel or financial advisers, drivers, and many others.

If the "technologists" are half-right, GDP will be much higher. So why should we not rejoice at the prospect of a 25- or 30-hour workweek and two months of annual leave, with intelligent machines taking up the slack?

Why, with all this new technology and imminent productivity increases, do so many continue to argue that everyone has to work more and retire much later in life if economies are to remain competitive? Or is it just the highly skilled who have to work harder and longer, because there are not enough of them? In that case, perhaps older workers should retire sooner to make room for the young, who have skills more appropriate to the new century. If such a shift were to increase overall GDP, fiscal transfers could pay for early retirement, while retirement itself could become a flexible and gradual process.

Finally, there is the question of climate change and possible natural-resource constraints, issues that have become more familiar over the last decade.[25] Will these factors impede long-term growth, or can a transition to a clean-energy economy fuel another technological revolution that actually increases prosperity?

As these questions move to the top of the policy agenda, it is becoming clearer that the traditional focus on growth, defined as an increase in aggregate GDP and calculated using national accounts invented a century ago, is less and less useful.

The nature and measurement of economic progress should involve a new social contract that allows societies to manage the power of technology so that it serves all citizens. Working, learning, enjoying leisure, and being healthy and "productive" should be part of a continuum in our lives, and policies should be explicitly aimed at what facilitates this continuum and increases measured well-being.

The trends underpinning widening inequality will have to be counteracted using many policy instruments, with tax regimes and life-long, inclusive, and affordable education and health care at the center of the effort to ensure equity and social mobility. Though the quality of human lives can still be greatly improved, even in the advanced countries, focusing on aggregate GDP will be less helpful in achieving this goal.

The questions surrounding future economic growth are becoming clearer. But we are only at the start of the process of creating the new conceptual framework needed to enable national and global policies to advance the cause of human progress.

December 16, 2014

THE OIL PRICE OPPORTUNITY

The sharp drop in the price of crude oil since late June has been grabbing headlines worldwide—and producing a lot of contradictory explanations.[26] Some attribute the fall largely to declining global growth expectations. Others focus on the expansion of America's oil and gas production. Still others suspect a tacit agreement between Saudi Arabia and the United States aimed at, among other things, weakening political rivals like Russia and Iran.

Regardless of the reason for the price drop—probably to be found in some combination of these factors—the consequences are the same. Though, as International Monetary Fund Managing Director Christine Lagarde has noted, lower oil prices may boost overall global growth, with the oil-importing advanced economies gaining the most, the impact on efforts to combat climate change could be devastating.

Indeed, a sustained decline in oil prices would not only make renewable energy sources less competitive now; it would impede their future competitiveness by discouraging research and investment. More generally, it would reduce the incentive for consumers, companies, and governments to pursue more energy-efficient practices.

Even if we remained on our current trajectory, keeping temperatures from rising more than 2° Celsius above pre-industrial levels—the threshold beyond which the most disruptive consequences of climate change would be triggered—would be next to impossible to achieve. As the UN's Intergovernmental Panel on Climate Change's most recent report reinforced, we cannot afford a slowdown in progress.[27]

Of course, climate science is not precise; instead, it works in terms of probability ranges. But uncertain estimates do not mean that the risk is any less acute. World leaders increasingly seem to recognize this in theory, including at the just-concluded climate change meeting in Lima, Peru.[28] But they continue to depend on nonbinding commitments—leaving the world on a dangerous climate trajectory.

A sharp decline in oil prices does, however, provide a rare political opportunity to introduce more carbon pricing. After all, one of the major arguments against a "carbon tax" has been that it would make energy more expensive. Even assurances that the revenue from such a tax would be refunded to taxpayers were inadequate to overcome political resistance, particularly in the United States.

But, with declining oil prices now exerting downward pressure on oil substitutes, a carbon tax could be introduced without raising the price of energy for consumers. Policymakers must simply be willing to forgo some of the short-term stimulus effects of cheaper energy. In fact, with low enough prices, consumers could still benefit from lower energy costs—just not quite as much as they are now.

The structure of a carbon-pricing scheme remains up for discussion. One option would be to introduce flexible pricing, tied to the price of oil. For example, for every $5 decline in the price per barrel, the carbon tax could be raised by a specified amount; for every $5 increase, the tax could be lowered by, say, two-thirds of that amount.

The carbon price would thus increase over time—the optimal outcome, according to growth models that account for climate constraints. At the same time, it would buffer consumers from oil-price volatility, thereby stabilizing their energy spending. Finally, and perhaps most important, such an approach would be more politically attractive than a fixed carbon tax, especially if it is introduced at a time of sharply declining oil prices.

In short, world leaders must take advantage of falling oil prices to move beyond indirect carbon pricing—achieved through the prices of carbon-emitting substances—to an explicit carbon tax that can help steer the world onto a more sustainable growth path. Crucially, in order to make a real impact, carbon-pricing schemes would have to be introduced in all major economies.

Of course, given the multitude of existing taxes, fees, and subsidies on energy products in various countries, the goal of aligning the effective cost of carbon with its most economically efficient level would take time to achieve. But introducing a modest, flexible carbon tax in major economies would be an important first step.

Today's environment of falling oil prices enables the world to take that step. It should be modest, so that it is politically feasible; flexible, so that it helps stabilize user prices; and it should increase over time, to place the global economy on a more sustainable path. Most important, it should be implemented quickly. After all, this window of opportunity will not remain open for very long.

April 17, 2015

CAN TRADE AGREEMENTS STOP CURRENCY MANIPULATION?

It is impossible to deny that trade and exchange rates are closely linked. But does that mean that international trade agreements should include provisions governing national policies that affect currency values?

Some economists certainly think so. Simon Johnson, for example, recently argued that mega-regional agreements like the Trans-Pacific Partnership should be used to discourage countries from intervening in the currency market to prevent exchange-rate appreciation; Fred Bergsten has made a similar argument.[29] But the United States Treasury and the Office of the U.S. Trade Representative continue to argue that macroeconomic issues should be kept separate from trade negotiations.

As it stands, the relevant international institutions—the World Trade Organization and the International Monetary Fund—are not organized to respond effectively to possible currency manipulation on their own. Incorporating macroeconomic policies affecting exchange rates into trade negotiations would require either that the WTO acquire the technical capacity (and mandate) to analyze and adjudicate relevant national policies or that the IMF join the dispute-settlement mechanisms that accompany trade treaties.

To be sure, since 2007, the IMF has prohibited "large-scale intervention in one direction in the exchange market," in a decision on "bilateral surveillance" that also identifies "large and prolonged" current-account imbalances as a reason for review.[30] But neither that decision nor later IMF policy papers on multilateral surveillance provide specific and comparative quantitative indicators that would eliminate the need for case-by-case judgment.[31]

The situation is complicated by the multitude of mechanisms whereby treasuries and central banks can drive down their exchange rates to gain a competitive trade advantage. The most direct method is purchases of foreign assets. But, in a world of large short-term capital flows, central bank policy interest rates—or even just announcements about likely future rates—also have a major impact. Moreover, quantitative easing affects exchange rates and trade, even if central banks purchase only domestic assets, as demonstrated by recent movements in the exchange rates of the dollar, the euro, and the yen.

One could go even further. An income-tax hike will reduce private demand (unless one believes in perfect Ricardian equivalence), including demand for other countries' exports.[32] Other macroeconomic policies of all kinds influence the current-account balance.

In short, for "policies affecting the exchange rate" to become part of trade agreements, monetary and fiscal policies would have to become part of trade agreements. In that case, there would be no trade agreements at all.

Consider the problem that would be posed by the Eurozone—an economy that faces major challenges in reconciling its members' divergent monetary, fiscal, and exchange-rate needs. Germany's current-account surplus has stood near 7% of GDP—bigger than China's—for two years, and is likely to grow even larger, owing to the euro's recent depreciation. Meanwhile, most other Eurozone countries have lately been forced to tighten fiscal policy, thereby reducing or eliminating their current-account deficits.

As a result, the total Eurozone trade surplus is now massive. Because individual Eurozone members have no monetary-policy tools at their disposal, the only way that Germany can reduce its surplus while remaining in the Eurozone is to conduct expansionary fiscal policy. The economist Stefan Kawalec has explicitly referred to the current policy mix in the Eurozone as "currency manipulation."[33]

Trade negotiations are hard enough to conclude. The need to wrestle with macroeconomic policy issues could easily cause talks to bog down—and give protectionist lobbies the political ammunition they need. That is why the Office of the U.S. Trade Representative is wisely trying not to add macroeconomic policy into the bargaining, despite demands from powerful voices in the U.S. Congress.

None of this means that macroeconomic policies that affect exchange rates are not problematic. They are. But trade negotiations are not the right forum for discussing the causes and consequences of current-account imbalances and reaching agreements on macroeconomic policy coordination; that is what the IMF and the G-20 are for. In fact, the issue of large actual or potential discrepancies between aggregate savings and investment in countries or monetary zones, reflected in current-account imbalances, is at the heart of the IMF's emerging multilateral surveillance role; it has been a focus of the G-20 as well.

The G-20 "mutual assessment process"—established to analyze national economic policies' effects on other countries and on global growth, with the goal of formulating individual adjustment commitments—has highlighted the difficulty of reaching agreement on macroeconomic policies with significant spillover effects. Indeed, it is even more difficult than reaching trade agreements, which must cover issues like tariffs, quotas, quality standards, regulatory regimes for particular sectors, and relevant microeconomic issues. Merging all of these challenging topics into a single negotiation process is a recipe for deadlock.

A better approach would include strengthening the IMF's multilateral surveillance role. Doing so would broaden discussions of macroeconomic policy to include employment issues—specifically, the potential impact of large foreign-trade surpluses on domestic jobs. And it would give trade negotiations a chance to succeed.

July 23, 2015

IS UBER A THREAT TO DEMOCRACY?

Every July, economists, business leaders, NGOs, and politicians from around the world gather in Aix-en-Provence, France, for the three-day Rencontres Économiques forum, organized by the Cercle des Économistes. This year's forum focused on the changing nature of work. The timing of the meeting, which coincided with a heated debate in France about the innovative ride-sharing service Uber, could not have been more apt.

The forum's theme was undoubtedly selected partly in response to fears that technological advances will lead to widespread unemployment, as machines become advanced enough to replace humans in performing an increasing number of tasks. As MIT's Andrew McAfee pointed out, historically, technological revolutions have "eventually led to more, if different, jobs."[34] But with machines becoming increasingly intelligent, "this time may be different."

Given this possibility, McAfee suggests, we may need to rebuild our societies so that, as intelligent machines increase productivity, the declining demand for human work has welfare-enhancing outcomes like higher (and more equitably distributed) incomes and more leisure time. He is not alone: John Maynard Keynes predicted this possibility 85 years ago.[35]

Uber, which enables people to connect with available drivers through a smartphone app, is precisely the kind of disruptive company that is driving the shift. Taxi drivers in France and around the world are particularly incensed about UberPOP (called UberX outside Europe), a no-frills service. Uber has since withdrawn UberPOP from France, at least temporarily—though not before two of its top managers were arrested for ignoring the government's injunction to suspend UberPOP.

But the kind of innovation that Uber exemplifies will not be stopped so easily.[36] Uber's software, in a sense, does the job of thousands of Walrasian auctioneers acting locally in space and time, leading to almost perfect price discrimination. Airlines have long employed such price discrimination, offering multiple prices for the same distance flown, depending on date and time. But Uber price setting is unique in its immediacy, which it has achieved by taking full advantage of modern communications technology.

In terms of work, Uber creates more jobs than it destroys. This leads to a clear increase in efficiency and provides overall income gains. Even if losers were fully compensated, the sum of the gains—shared by the firm, its mostly part-time workers, and its customers—would far outweigh the losses.

Nevertheless, there are real problems that must be addressed. For starters, there are the losers: traditional taxi drivers, who often have had to pay large license fees and thus cannot compete with Uber's low prices. While this problem always arises when disruptive new technologies appear, innovation and adoption are occurring faster than ever. Taxi drivers are being asked to adjust in a matter of days, rather than years, leaving democratic systems little time to determine how much compensation they should receive, and how it should be distributed.

Another problem is regulation. Taxis produce not only income tax, but also value-added or sales taxes. But the UberPOP software, at least so far, has made it impossible to collect value-added tax. To level the playing field, local or national authorities should require the company to integrate tax-collection software into its app. The fact that UberPOP drivers, unlike taxi drivers, do not cover passenger insurance also amounts to unfair competition, and must be remedied.

Moreover, in France, taxi drivers must undergo regular

health and professional tests, to which UberPOP drivers are not subject. Like all Uber drivers, they are "monitored" by users, who evaluate them through the app after each ride. This may be a useful innovation; but it is not really a valid replacement for, say, an eye exam.

The final problem with innovative companies like Uber is that the financial returns overwhelmingly accrue to the company's leadership, rather than to the service providers. Whether or not that is justified, such companies' contribution to rising income inequality—and thus to regulatory capture, media bias, and disproportionate influence in elections—cannot be ignored.

Uber is just one example of disruptive innovation that brings huge increases in efficiency, as well as real social and regulatory challenges, a point that French Economy Minister Emmanuel Macron emphasized in his speech at Rencontres Économiques. And, in fact, Uber is one of the less problematic innovations, because it is a net job creator; the rise of computers capable of replacing call-center workers, by contrast, is resulting in large net job losses. In a democratic system, the challenges that such disruptive technologies bring must be confronted in a way that ensures fairness, without impeding progress.

The creative destruction of the so-called second machine age cannot and should not be stopped. But to think that markets alone can manage its transformative impact is pure folly—a fact that the recent global economic crisis, which was rooted in unbridled financial innovation, made clear. What is needed now are new social and regulatory policies, often global in nature, that embody a new social contract for the 21st century.[37]

PART II

THE SOCIAL CONTRACT, PUBLIC POLICY, AND INEQUALITY

Millions of citizens making up most nations generally and rather amazingly comply with the laws and regulations governing them. Governments do of course have coercive powers. But in reasonably well-functioning democracies, these powers are used in limited ways. Social and political cohesion endures because governments are broadly perceived as legitimate, and the relationship between public institutions and citizens is based on a "social contract." This social contract is partly enshrined in constitutions and laws; but it also exists de facto in people's attitudes and behavior. It has to be based on a sense of fairness, a sense of security, and a sense of community. Even authoritarian governments cannot endure for very long if there is no perceived social contract.

The social contract that had evolved in most democracies is increasingly challenged today by the more engulfing form globalization has taken, and the mind-boggling pace of technological change. Both forces coalesce to create a constant need for new learning as well as a more fragmented economic production system. This creates more uncertainty and a greater need for individuals to adapt, which many find difficult, particularly if they cannot build on an education that has prepared them for continuous learning. Moreover the increasing and new forms of inequality that have accompanied these trends challenge the basic notion of fairness, or indeed of "tradition," on which a social contract has to be based. It is not necessarily inequality itself that is always the greatest problem, but its nature and the perceived lack of fairness. I doubt that many begrudge top performing brain surgeons their considerable income. But pre-negotiated golden parachutes of many millions of dollars for executives who get fired for lack of performance are simply incomprehensible when there are so many workers who have to accept lower wages or lose their jobs. The worrisome rise of sectarian identity politics is testimony to weaker perceived legitimacy of governing institutions and widespread frustration.

Attempts at describing what is needed for a new social contract in tune with our century, the multilevel nature of public policy, and the problems of inequality constitute the core topics of Part II of this collection of essays. Recalling the key theme of Part I, issues surrounding the social contract, inequality, and the nature of public policy all need an *international* perspective. Thomas Piketty in his amazing and erudite bestseller on the nature of inequality ends up proposing a rather impractical global tax on wealth as a solution.[38] This illustrates how limited purely national public policy seems to have become.

Public policy must be described, analyzed, and reformed at multiple levels: local, subregional, city and metropolitan level, national, continental (for example, the European Union), and global. It really no longer makes much sense to argue about public policy without specifying what levels of governance the debate should focus on.

Part II includes an essay describing the difficulty of "being in the political center" in democratic politics. It was inspired at the time of writing by the challenges a world class "super-technocrat" like Mario Monti faced when he tried to become an Italian politician. It may be that 70% of citizens in a country feel that centrist solutions are the most desirable ones. Political dynamics are such, however, that strong commitment and strong beliefs, translating into strong activism, favor those who can rally the "troops" of the left or of the right. This rarely allows the emergence of a majority center party. When such parties exceptionally succeed, they tend not to last.

Somewhat paradoxically, it may be both easier and better for democracy, and general moderation, if the leadership of the left and of the right can fully integrate those leaning further left and further right into large center-left and center-right coalitions, rather than have a center trying to emerge squeezed between stronger extremes. The strength of many successful democracies, including for example, until recently at least, the American and German ones, has been exactly the ability of the center right and the center left to integrate a broad spectrum and thus marginalize the extremes.

The breakdown of the old social contract may today endanger this stabilizing feature of democratic politics. It may actually create a new opening for political centrists, but it is more likely to lead to greater polarization and more political fragmentation. In 2015 and 2016 we have observed such polarization and fragmentation gain momentum.

The success of Thomas Piketty's book and many other events, such as the ability of a self-described socialist to attract large number of young voters in the United States, but also the political reflexes of parts of the far right, particularly in Europe, underline the importance increasing inequality has taken in the public debate. Several essays in Part II discuss the link between inequality and technology, including one, "The Great Income Divide," which notes that Piketty's dynamic rule of today's capitalism—the increasing share of profits—depends crucially on the degree of substitutability of capital for labor.[39] The new social contract proposed in another essay emphasizes the need to design renewed social insurance and protection arrangements so that they fully address the needs created by irreversible technological change.

How exactly technology will evolve and what kind of new jobs will emerge is almost, by definition, unknowable. It is quite certain, however, that economic activity in 2030 will be very different in nature and structure than it is today. The social arrangements that make up the social contract will have to adapt. Politics, locally and globally, can and should facilitate these changes, not by prescribing blueprints that may turn out to be unworkable, but by encouraging an inclusive dialogue and looking for wherever best practice seems to be succeeding to scale it up at all levels of governance. Political economy at the time of the digital revolution points to the need for experimentation and coherence, caution and courage. The most successful societies will be those that find the right balance between both requirements.

THE INEQUALITY TRAP

As evidence mounts that income inequality is increasing in many parts of the world, the problem has received growing attention from academics and policymakers. In the United States, for example, the income share of the top 1% of the population has more than doubled since the late 1970s, from about 8% of annual GDP to more than 20% recently, a level not reached since the 1920s.

While there are ethical and social reasons to worry about inequality, they do not have much to do with macroeconomic policy per se. But such a link was seen in the early part of the 20th century: capitalism, some argued, tends to generate chronic weakness in effective demand due to growing concentration of income, leading to a "savings glut," because the very rich save a lot. This would spur "trade wars" as countries tried to find more demand abroad.

From the late 1930s onward, however, this argument faded as the market economies of the West grew rapidly in the post–World War II period and income distributions became more equal. While there was a business cycle, no perceptible tendency toward chronic demand weakness appeared. Short-term interest rates, most macroecono-

mists would say, could always be set low enough to generate reasonable rates of employment and demand.

Now, however, with inequality on the rise once more,
arguments linking income concentration to macroeconomic
problems have returned. The University of Chicago's Ra-
ghuram Rajan, a former chief economist at the International
Monetary Fund, tells a plausible story in his recent award-
winning book, *Fault Lines*, about the connection between
income inequality and the financial crisis of 2008.

Rajan argues that huge income concentration at the top
in the United States led to policies aimed at encouraging
unsustainable borrowing by lower- and middle-income
groups, through subsidies and loan guarantees in the housing sector and loose monetary policy. There was also an
explosion of credit-card debt. These groups protected the
growth in consumption to which they had become accustomed by going more deeply into debt. Indirectly, the very
rich, some of them outside the United States, lent to the
other income groups, with the financial sector intermedi-
ating in aggressive ways. This unsustainable process came
to a crashing halt in 2008.

Joseph Stiglitz in his book *Freefall* and Robert Reich in
his *Aftershock* have told similar stories, while the economists Michael Kumhof and Romain Ranciere have devised
a formal mathematical version of the possible link between
income concentration and financial crisis. While the underlying models differ, the Keynesian versions emphasize
that if the super-rich save a lot, ever-increasing income concentration can be expected to lead to a chronic excess of
planned savings over investment.

Macroeconomic policy can try to compensate through

deficit spending and very low interest rates. Or an undervalued exchange rate can help to export the lack of domestic demand. But if the share of the highest income groups keeps rising, the problem will remain chronic. And, at some point, when public debt has become too large to allow continued deficit spending, or when interest rates are close to their zero lower bound, the system runs out of solutions.

This story has a counterintuitive dimension. Is it not the case that the problem in the United States has been too little savings, rather than too much? Doesn't the country's persistent current-account deficit reflect excessive consumption, rather than weak effective demand?

The recent work by Rajan, Stiglitz, Kumhof and Ranciere, and others explains the apparent paradox: those at the very top financed the demand of everyone else, which enabled both high employment levels and large current-account deficits. When the crash came in 2008, massive fiscal and monetary expansion prevented U.S. consumption from collapsing. But did it cure the underlying problem?

Although the dynamics leading to increased income concentration have not changed, it is no longer easy to borrow, and in that sense another boom-and-bust cycle is unlikely. But that raises another difficulty. When asked why they do not invest more, most firms cite insufficient demand. But how can domestic demand be strong if income continues to flow to the top?

Consumption demand for luxury goods is unlikely to solve the problem. Moreover, interest rates cannot become negative in nominal terms, and rising public debt may increasingly disable fiscal policy. So, if the dynamics fueling income concentration cannot be reversed, the super-rich save a large fraction of their income, luxury goods cannot fuel sufficient demand, lower-income groups can no longer borrow, fiscal and monetary policies have reached their limits, and unemployment cannot be exported, an economy may become stuck.

The early 2012 upturn in U.S. economic activity still owes a lot to extraordinarily expansionary monetary policy and unsustainable fiscal deficits. If income concentration could be reduced as the budget deficit was reduced, demand could be financed by sustainable, broad-based private incomes. Public debt could be reduced without fear of recession, because private demand would be stronger. Investment would increase as demand prospects improved.

This line of reasoning is particularly relevant to the United States, given the extent of income concentration and the fiscal challenges that lie ahead. But the broad trend toward larger income shares at the top is global, and the difficulties that it may create for macroeconomic policy should no longer be ignored.

July 20, 2012

WHAT ROLE FOR THE STATE?

The financial crisis of 2008 has spurred a global debate on how much government regulation of markets—and what kind—is appropriate. In the United States, it is a key theme in the upcoming presidential election, and it is shaping politics in Europe and emerging markets as well.

For starters, China's impressive growth performance over the last three decades has given the world an economically successful example of what many call "state capitalism." Brazil's development policies have also accorded a strong role to the state.

Questions concerning the state's size and the sustainable role of government are central to the debate over the Eurozone's fate as well. Many critics of Europe, particularly in the United States, link the euro crisis to the outsize role of government there, though the Scandinavian countries are doing well despite high public spending. In France, the new center-left government faces the challenge of delivering on its promise of strengthening social solidarity while substantially reducing the budget deficit.

Alongside the mostly economic arguments about the role of government, many countries are experiencing widespread disillusionment with politics and a growing distance between citizens and government (particularly national government). In many countries, participation rates in national elections are falling, and new parties and movements, such as the Pirate Party in Germany and the Five Star Movement in Italy, reflect strong discontent with existing governance.

In the United States, the approval rating of Congress reached a record low of 14% in 2015. Many experienced analysts, such as my colleague Bruce Katz at the Brookings Institution, believe that the only solution is to bring a larger share of governance and policy initiation to the state and municipal level, in close partnership with the private sector and civil society.

But that approach, too, might have a downside. Consider Spain, where too much fiscal decentralization to regional governments contributed significantly to weakening otherwise strong public finances.

A crucial problem for this global debate is that, despite the realities of 21st-century technology and globalization, it is still conducted largely as if governance and public policy were almost exclusively the domain of the nation-state. To adapt the debate to the real challenges that we face, we should focus on four levels of governance and identify the most appropriate allocation of public-policy functions to them.

First, many policies—including support for local infrastructure, land zoning, facilitation of industrial production and training, traffic ordinances, and environmental regulations—can largely be determined at the local or metropolitan level and reflect the wishes of a local electorate.

Of course, defense and foreign policy will continue to be conducted primarily at the second level—the nation-state. Most nation-states maintain national currencies and must therefore pursue fiscal and economic policies that support a monetary union. As the Eurozone crisis has starkly reminded us, decentralization cannot extend too far into the budgetary sphere, lest it threaten the common currency's survival.

The U.S. system is manageable, because the American states are largely constrained to running balanced budgets, while the federal government accounts for most fiscal policy. Moreover, banking regulation and deposit insurance are centralized in the United States, as they must be in a monetary union. The Eurozone has finally recognized this.

So, governance at the nation-state level remains hugely important and is intimately linked to monetary sovereignty. The key problem in Europe today is whether Eurozone members will advance toward something resembling a federal nation-state. Unless they do, it is difficult to see how the common currency can survive.

There is also a third, regional or continental, level of governance, which is most advanced in the European Union (and is being tested in Latin America, Africa, and Asia) and can be very useful. Customs unions, free-trade areas, or a single market, as in Europe, allow greater mobility of goods and services, which can lead to benefits from economies of scale that remaining trade impediments at the global level do not permit. Europe's borderless Schengen area is another example of regional supranational governance. There are also aspects of infrastructure that can best be addressed at the continental level.

Finally, there is the global level. The spread of infectious disease, global trade and finance, climate change, nuclear nonproliferation, counterterrorism, and cyber security are just some of the issues that require broad international cooperation and global governance.

In today's interdependent world, the debate about the role of public policy, the size and functions of government, and the legitimacy of public decisionmaking should be conducted with the four levels of governance much more clearly in focus. The levels often will overlap (infrastructure and clean energy issues, for example), but democracy could be greatly strengthened if the issues were linked to the levels at which decisions can best be taken.

As Pascal Lamy, the director of the World Trade Organization, has said, it is not only the "local" that has to be brought to the "global"; the inherently "local" political sphere must internalize the global or regional context. That is a huge challenge for political leadership and communication, but if it is not met, democracy and globalization will be difficult to reconcile. How to conduct democratic debate with reference to these local, national, continental, and global levels, and to structure a political space that better reflects economic and social space, will be the great challenge of the decades ahead.

January 14, 2013

THE CENTRISTS CANNOT HOLD

In most advanced democracies, a large center-right party competes with a large center-left party. Of course, the extent to which an electoral system favors large parties—by requiring high popular-vote thresholds to enter parliament or through winner-take-all constituencies—affects the degree of political fragmentation. But, by and large, the developed democracies are characterized by competition between large parties on the center left and center right. What, then, are true centrists like Mario Monti, Italy's respected technocratic prime minister, to do?

To be sure, regional and ethnic allegiances play a greater role in some places in Europe—for example, Scotland, Belgium, and Catalonia—but far more so in emerging countries where political cleavages also reflect specific postcolonial circumstances and often the legacy of single-party rule. Nonetheless, even in emerging-market democracies, such as Chile, Mexico, South Korea, and India, a left-right cleavage plays an important role—while those who claim the political center generally remain weak.

The British Liberal Democrats, for example, have tried for decades to become a strong centrist third party, without success. While the political vocabulary in the United States is different, the Democratic Party, since Franklin Roosevelt's presidency, is indeed a center-left force, the Republican Party occupies the right, and no other significant party exists.

In France and Germany, there is more fragmentation. Politics is still dominated by a large center-left party and a large center-right party, but smaller groups—some claiming the center and others the right and left extremes—challenge them to various degrees. In some countries, the "Greens" have their own identity, close to the left; but, despite remarkable progress in Germany, they remain unable to reach the electoral size of the large center-right and center-left parties.

Variations of this basic structure exist in Spain, Portugal, Greece, Turkey, and the Nordic countries. The situation is particularly interesting in Italy, where Monti, having decided to contest the upcoming general election, has had to position himself on the right (which he signaled by attending a gathering of the leaders of Europe's center-right parties). He and former Prime Minister Silvio Berlusconi are now fighting for space on the right, with the center-left Democrats leading in the polls.

There are at least four differences between center-right

and center-left approaches to social and economic challenges. The right has greater confidence in markets to allocate resources and provide appropriate incentives; favors private consumption over public goods; is minimally concerned with economic inequality; and tends to be more nationalistic and less optimistic about international cooperation.

The left, by contrast, believes that markets, particularly financial markets, need considerable government regulation and supervision to function well; gives greater weight to public goods (for example, parks, a clean environment, and mass-transit systems); seeks to reduce economic inequality, believing that it undermines democracy and the sense of fairness that is important to well-being; and is more willing to pursue international cooperation as a means to secure peace and provide global public goods, such as climate protection.

When looking at actual economic policies as they have evolved over decades, we see that they always combine center-right and center-left elements. Repeated financial crises have tempered even the right's faith in unregulated markets, while the left has become more realistic and cautious about state planning and bureaucratic processes. Likewise, the choice between privately consumed and publicly consumed "goods" is often blurred, as politicians tend to reinforce citizens' understandable tendency to demand public goods while rejecting the taxes needed to pay for them.

As income inequality has increased—dramatically in some countries, such as the United States—it is moving to the forefront of the debate, reinforcing the traditional political divide. Nonetheless, the center right and the center left are arguing about the degree of redistribution, not about the need for some progressivity in taxes and transfers. Both also agree on the need for international cooperation in an increasingly interdependent world, with differences mainly concerning how much effort to spend on it.

So, given that differences in policies as they are implemented have become largely a matter of degree, why do centrist parties remain weak? Why have they failed to unite moderates on both sides of the ideological divide?

One reason is that only a minority of any population is active politically. Active party members hold more ideologically consistent views—and hold them more strongly—than most of those who are politically less engaged, giving activists disproportionate influence in the political process. After all, more nuanced ideas and policy proposals are relatively difficult to propagate effectively enough to generate broad and enthusiastic popular support.

But there also really are fundamental differences in values and economic philosophies, as well as in economic interests, leading to a fairly consistent positioning of voters on the right or left. Disagreement may lead to compromises, but that does not change the underlying differences in starting positions.

It is probably a good thing that structured competition between large center-right and center-left parties persists. Such parties can help to integrate the extremes into the political mainstream, while facilitating alternation in power, which is essential to any democracy's dynamism; a system in which a large centrist party remained permanently in power would be far less desirable. Those, like Monti, who want to mount a challenge from the center, however personally impressive they may be, have steep obstacles to overcome, and for good reasons.

April 15, 2013

ECONOMIC POLICY'S NARRATIVE IMPERATIVE

The best advice I received when taking up policymaking responsibilities in Turkey more than a decade ago was to take "a lot of time and care to develop and communicate the 'narrative' to support the policy program that you want to succeed." The more that economic policy is subject to public debate—that is, the more democracy there is—the more important such policy narratives are.

The crisis faced by the European Union and the Eurozone is a telling example of the need for a narrative that explains public policy and generates political support for it. A successful narrative can be neither too complicated nor simplistic. It must capture the imagination, address the public's anxieties, and generate realistic hope. Voters often sense cheap populism.

European Central Bank President Mario Draghi provided such a narrative to the financial markets last July. He said that the ECB would do everything necessary to prevent the disintegration of the euro, adding simply: "Believe me, it will be enough."

With that sentence, Draghi eliminated the perceived re-denomination tail risk that was highest in the case of

Greece, but that was driving up borrowing costs in Spain, Italy, and Portugal as well. It was not a populist message, because the ECB does indeed have the firepower to buy enough sovereign bonds on the secondary market to put a ceiling on interest rates, at least for many months. Central bankers, more generally, are typically able to provide short- or medium-term narratives to financial markets. U.S. Federal Reserve Board Chairman Ben Bernanke provided his own by pledging that U.S. short-term interest rates would remain very low, and the Bank of Japan's new chairman, Haruhiko Kuroda, has just provided another by saying that he will double the money supply so that inflation reaches 2%.

While central bankers can provide such narratives to financial markets, it is political leaders who must provide the overall socioeconomic messages that encourage long-term real investment, deliver electoral support for reform, and hope for the future. Central bank alchemy, to borrow a term from American journalist Neil Irwin's new book, *The Alchemists: Three Central Bankers and a World on Fire*, has its limits.[40]

Europe, in particular, needs a narrative of long-term hope that will trigger a real recovery. France is coming closer to the danger zone, and even Germany's annual GDP growth is falling well below 1% per year. In the meantime, the easing of sovereign interest-rate spreads provides little comfort to the growing army of unemployed in southern Europe, where youth unemployment has reached dramatic heights—close to 60% in Greece and Spain, and almost 40% in Italy.

The narrative should address three essential questions.

How can the European model of strong social solidarity and security be reformed, but endure? How can economic growth be revived and sustained throughout the EU? And how can Europe's institutions function with enhanced legitimacy to accommodate countries that share the euro and others that retain their national currencies?

For starters, a revolution is required in the organization of work, learning, and leisure. Social solidarity, essential to European identity, can and must include longer work lives, but also more work sharing, adult learning, and shorter average work weeks (particularly close to retirement).

Such flexibility requires the consent of all: employees must adjust to changing requirements; employers must reorganize their enterprises to allow more work sharing, work from home, and learning intervals; and governments must overhaul taxes, income support, and regulation to promote a "flex-solidarity revolution" that encourages personal choice and responsibility, while remaining committed to social cohesion. This can lead to a better future for all, with citizens gaining better access to adult education, having more free time to pursue personal interests, and remaining productive and occupationally engaged far longer into their healthy lives.

Europe does not need Asia's rates of economic growth. It can secure decent jobs and prosperity, with a sustained annual growth rate of around 2%. To achieve that, German voters should be told not that their country's resources will forever flow to Spain, but that their wages can rise at twice the rate of the recent past without risking inflation or a current-account deficit, because Germany has the world's largest external surplus.

Service-sector industries throughout the EU must be opened up. The countries with stronger fiscal positions should take the lead in a major pan-European skill-upgrading program. The number of pan-European scholarships should be doubled. School programs everywhere should aim to educate trilingual citizens.

Moreover, a full European banking union with shared resources for resolution should be created without further delay. The European Investment Bank, which received a significant capital increase in 2012, should add a large investment-support program for medium-size enterprises to its current operations, with a subsidy financed from the European budget to encourage first-time job takers for a limited period. Jobs and training for young people must be the centerpiece for the new growth pact, and projects must move ahead in "crisis mode," rather than according to business as usual.

Finally, while monetary union obviously requires greater sharing of sovereignty, there should also be a "greater Europe" that includes the United Kingdom and others. This implies two-tier institutions that can accommodate both types of countries: the "euro-ins" and those that prefer to preserve their monetary sovereignty in a larger Europe built around a vibrant single market and common democratic values.

These interconnected visions can and must be realized if Europe is to thrive again. Together, they form a compelling narrative that European leaders must begin to articulate.

May 10, 2013

BALANCING THE TECHNOCRATS

A simplistic (actually, naive) view of markets is that they exist almost in a "state of nature," and that the best of all worlds is one where they are free to operate without government interference. An equally simplistic view of democracy is that it is a political system in which periodic competitive elections give the winner the right to govern without constraint.

The reality is far more complex, of course. Markets can function only within an institutional and legal framework that includes property rights, enforcement of contracts, quality and information controls, and many other rules to govern transactions.

Similarly, while competitive elections are essential to any democratic system, a "winner-take-all" attitude to electoral outcomes, with the victor concentrating power, is incompatible with democracy in the long term. Well-functioning democracies are embedded in complex constitutional and other laws that separate executive, legislative, and judicial power, and that protect freedom of speech, assembly, and peaceful dissent by those who lose elections.

Regulatory institutions—such as bank supervisory agencies and bodies that oversee the telecommunications, food, and energy industries—play a vital role by maintaining the always-delicate balance between "free" markets and the actions of elected governments and legislatures. The central bank is perhaps the most important of these institutions, for it conducts monetary policy (and sometimes serves as the financial-sector regulator).

The policy and regulatory mistakes that contributed to the subprime mortgage crisis—and thus to the U.S. financial system's near-meltdown and the Eurozone's travails—have brought the issue of optimal economic regulation and its relation to democracy to the fore once again. In the United States, a significant share of Republican Party members favor abolishing not only the Department of Energy and the Environmental Protection Agency, but also the Federal Reserve! In their view, markets and private initiative require no significant regulation. The role of politics is to elect majorities that can abolish regulations and regulatory bodies.

Others around the world similarly oppose regulatory institutions, but for very different reasons. They argue that politicians can regulate and supervise without intermediate bodies that have some degree of autonomy. In their minds, these bodies merely impede and constrain realization of the people's will. If an elected government wants a bank to offer cheap credit to a group of enterprises so that they can hire more people, why should a supervisor be able to obstruct this democratic will? If these enterprises are told to hire the governing party's supporters as an implicit condition of obtaining subsidized credit, that, too, is the expression of electorally legitimized popular will.

At the other end of the spectrum are technocratic super-defenders of regulatory bodies who believe that politicians and electorates are hopelessly confused, uneducated, and often corrupt. Management of the economy should be entrusted to competent and independent experts, a group of "Platonic Guardians" empowered to act in the state's higher interests, regardless of electoral outcomes or public opinion.

The International Monetary Fund, the European Commission, and the European Central Bank are often viewed as such technocratic institutions—and as supporting the technocratic element within states and societies around the world. At the height of the Eurozone crisis, the IMF, the EC, and the ECB (not to mention financial markets) warmly welcomed the economists Mario Monti and Lucas Papademos as highly respected technocratic prime ministers for Italy and Greece, respectively.

Experience in recent decades has shown that a balanced and "moderate" approach is needed on these matters. Electoral cycles (and the accompanying political pressures) are such that monetary policy, banking, and many other areas of policy and economic activity must be overseen by those with professional competence and a much longer time horizon than that of politicians.

Day-to-day politics cannot dominate the regulation that markets need. The single most important institutional reform underlying price stability throughout the world has been the stronger independence of central banks. But, if independent technocrats are allowed to determine long-term policy and set objectives that cannot be influenced by democratic majorities, democracy itself is in serious jeopardy. I find it undemocratic, for example, that the ECB can set the Eurozone-wide inflation target unilaterally. How much inflation a society finds desirable or tolerable (taking into account other important variables, such as employment, GDP growth, or poverty) is an inherently political question that should be debated in parliament. The central bank should be consulted, but its role should be to implement the objective without political interference: independence in terms of policy tools, not goals.

Globalization and the increasing complexity of financial and other markets make it imperative that the domains of private activity, political decisionmaking, and regulation be clarified. The challenge is even greater because some regulatory agencies must be multilateral, or at least intergovernmental, given the global nature of much economic activity. The difference and the distance between markets and politics must be clear—and, for the sake of both effectiveness and legitimacy, it must be based on rules that are well understood and on popular consent.

July 18, 2013

THE NEXT SOCIAL CONTRACT

Around the world nowadays, persistent unemployment, skill mismatches, and retirement frameworks have become central to fiscal policy—and to the often-fierce political debates that surround it. The advanced countries are facing an immediate "aging" problem, but most of the emerging economies are also in the midst of a demographic transition that will result in an age structure similar to that of the advanced economies—that is, an inverted pyramid—in just two or three decades. Indeed, China will get there much sooner.

Multiple problems affect employment. Weak demand in the aftermath of the global financial crisis that began in 2008 remains a key factor in Europe, the United States, and Japan. But longer-term structural issues are weighing down labor markets as well.

Most important, globalization results in a continuous shift of comparative advantage, creating serious adjustment problems as employment created in new activities does not necessarily compensate for the loss of jobs in old ones. In any case, most new jobs require different skills, implying that workers losing their jobs in dying industries have little hope of finding others.

Moreover, technological progress is becoming ever more "labor-saving," with computers and robots replacing human workers in settings ranging from supermarkets to automobile assembly lines. Given the volatile macroeconomic outlook, many firms are reluctant to hire new workers, leading to high youth unemployment throughout the world.

At the same time, aging—and the associated cost of health care for the elderly—constitutes the main fiscal challenge in maturing societies. By the middle of this century, life expectancy at age 60 will have risen by about ten years relative to the post–World War II period, when current retirement ages were fixed.

Marginal changes to existing arrangements are unlikely to be sufficient to respond to technological forces, reduce social tensions and young people's fears, or address growing fiscal burdens. A radical reassessment of work, skill formation, retirement, and leisure is needed, with several principles forming the core of any comprehensive reform.

For starters, skill formation and development must become a lifelong process, starting with formal schooling, but continuing through on-the-job training and intervals of full-time education at different points in life. Special youth insertion programs should become a normal part of public support for employment and career formation, with exemption from social security contributions for the first one or two years of employment.

A second principle is that retirement should be a gradual process. People could work an average of 1,800-2,000 hours per year until they reach their 50s, taper off to 1,300-1,500 hours in their early 60s, and move toward the 500-1,000 range as they approach 70. A hospital nurse, an airplane crew member, or a secondary-school teacher, for example, could work five days a week until her late fifties, four days a week until age 62, three days until age 65, and perhaps two days until age 70.

Employers and workers should negotiate such flexibility, but they should do so with incentives and financial support from government—for example, variable social security and income taxes. Paid holidays can be three to four weeks until age 45, gradually increasing to seven to eight weeks in one's late 60s. Maternity and paternity leave should be increased where it is low, such as in the United States.

Public policies should also encourage greater scope for individual choice. For example, every ten years, a worker should be able to engage in a year of formal learning, with one-third of the cost paid by the employer, one-third by public funds, and one-third by personal savings (these proportions could vary by income bracket).

The overall objective should be a society in which, health permitting, citizens work and pay taxes until close to the age of 70, but less intensively with advancing age and in a flexible manner that reflects individual circumstances. In fact, gradual and flexible retirement would in many cases benefit not only employers and governments, but also workers themselves, because continued occupational engagement is often a source of personal satisfaction and emotionally enriching social interaction.

Using the Gallup World Poll, my colleagues at the Brookings Institution in Washington, D.C., Carol Graham and Milena Nikolova, have found that the happiest cohorts are those who work part-time voluntarily. In exchange for longer work lives, citizens would have more time for both leisure and skill formation throughout their lives, with positive effects on productivity and life satisfaction.

The new social contract for the first half of the 21st century must be one that combines fiscal realism, significant room for individual preferences, and strong social solidarity and protection against shocks stemming from personal circumstances or a volatile economy. Many countries are taking steps in this direction. They are too timid. We need a comprehensive and revolutionary reframing of education, work, retirement, and leisure time.

January 9, 2014

THE GREAT WAR AND GLOBAL GOVERNANCE

This year marks the 100th anniversary of the outbreak of World War I—and, arguably, the worst year in human history. A century later, is the world any safer?

Not only did WWI leave almost 40 million people dead, it can be viewed as a precursor to World War II.

After all, had Germany's hyperinflation of the 1920s—a direct result of the war—been avoided, Hitler may well never have risen to power, and WWII might not have occurred. Instead, the assassination of Austrian Archduke Franz Ferdinand in Sarajevo on June 28, 1914, set in motion a chain of bloodletting that killed nearly 100 million people by 1945 and caused human suffering on a previously unimaginable scale.

Of course, generations of historians have meticulously researched the origins of the world wars and written elegantly about their conclusions.[41] That history should spur today's economists and policymakers to reflect on the difficult trade-off between efficiency and robustness when it comes to global governance.

The painstaking effort since the end of WWII to build effective regional and global governance institutions has reduced considerably the risk of catastrophes like the world wars or the Great Depression. Indeed, while such institutions are far from perfect, the progress that has been made in terms of preventing human suffering is worth far more than the efficiency costs of ensuring that they are adequately robust.

This efficiency-robustness trade-off exists in many fields. When designing an airplane, aeronautical engineers must ensure sufficient robustness so that their creation can avoid crashing even under highly unusual or unforeseen circumstances. This requires a degree of redundancy—for example, extra engines and extensive backup systems—that comes at the cost of efficiency.

Economic systems also must be robust, as episodes like the Great Depression or the 2008 global financial crisis demonstrate. In the United States, in particular, the financial sector's structure prior to the recent crisis emphasized the efficient generation of huge profits—and succeeded for more than a decade. But the realization in 2007 that some of the system's fundamental assumptions were no longer valid triggered a crisis with huge economic and social costs. Had governments worldwide not intervened with massive rescue and stimulus packages, the consequences would have been catastrophic.

That near miss highlighted the unsustainability of precrisis policies. The new Basel III banking guidelines,[42] together with new national regulations, aim at creating a more robust financial system by insisting on higher capital-adequacy ratios, less leverage, greater separation between investment and retail banking, a better macroprudential framework, and measures to prevent financial institutions from becoming "too big to fail." Minimizing the risk of a major war, depression, or financial breakdown thus requires that policymakers find the optimal balance—and that requires more explicit discussion of the efficiency-robustness trade-off.

All of these efforts are shaped by the efficiency-robustness trade-off. If capital requirements are pushed too high, banks become less profitable, making it more difficult for them to channel savings to investment and undermining economic growth. The challenge, therefore, is to find the ideal balance between opportunity and security—that is, between efficiency and robustness.

Policymakers face a similar challenge when designing, for example, efforts to combat climate change. The scientific consensus is that greenhouse-gas emissions are generating significant risks, but the scale and timing of these risks remain uncertain.

To illustrate the trade-off (in admittedly simplistic terms), a 14% capital-adequacy ratio for banks may be compared to the objective of stabilizing carbon-dioxide levels in the atmosphere at 450 parts per million, with both targets reflecting caution and a desire for robustness, at an immediate economic cost. By contrast, a capital-adequacy target of 7% and a CO_2 target of 550 ppm would demonstrate policymakers' willingness to place a higher priority on short-term gains—even if that means allowing another financial crisis or global warming's long-term economic and human consequences to manifest themselves.

An extreme course in either direction would be a bad idea. After all, it is impossible to avoid all risk, and, at a certain point, the level of inefficiency generated by excessive robustness would create new risks of collapse.

As it stands, policies are often presented without any mention of costs in terms of efficiency or robustness—and mere awareness of the trade-off is insufficient for effective decisionmaking. Instead, the trade-off must be quantified in approximate and reasonably accessible terms to facilitate productive debate and preempt polarized ideological clashes that have little hope of resolution.

Perhaps the commemoration this year of the disaster unleashed in 1914 will inspire people to think more deeply about how to avoid major risks without having to pay a prohibitively high price in lost efficiency and dynamism to ensure robustness and resilience. Now, as then, the fate of the world hangs in the balance.

March 13, 2014

GOOD GOVERNANCE AND
ECONOMIC PERFORMANCE

The debate about emerging countries' growth prospects is now in full swing. Pessimists stress the feared reversal of private capital flows, owing to the U.S. Federal Reserve's tapering of its purchases of long-term assets, as well as the difficulties of so-called second- and third-generation structural reforms and the limits to "catch-up" growth outside of manufacturing. Optimists argue that the potential for rapid growth remains immense, owing to better macroeconomic fundamentals and the promise of best-practice technology spreading throughout the emerging world.

So who is right?

Recent events point once again to the importance of good governance and responsive political systems, a familiar topic in studies of long-term economic growth. Countries that appeared successful for a long time, such as Turkey or Thailand, suddenly seem to face obstacles related to governance and the ability to forge domestic political compromises. The resulting divisiveness and dysfunction are surely bigger threats than the Fed's tapering.

It is the nature of governance that determines whether people deploy their talents and energy in pursuit of innovation, production, and job creation, or in rent seeking and lobbying for political protection. And here the contrast between Egypt and Tunisia may turn out to be an object lesson in what makes the difference between success and failure.

In Egypt, the old regime under Hosni Mubarak, having failed to democratize, collapsed in the face of massive protest. A low-turnout election gave a plurality of the popular vote to the Muslim Brotherhood, which came to power alone and proceeded to ignore good governance and alienate all except its most fervent followers.

The Brotherhood's approach to governance also explains the mess it made of the economy. Instead of trying to build nonpartisan and competent regulatory institutions, all positions were stacked with political followers. Unfortunately, the military intervention last July gave rise to yet another regime that seems unable to build durable institutions that could foster political reconciliation and deliver inclusive growth.

Tunisia may give us an example of the opposite scenario: a real constitutional compromise supported by an overwhelming majority (reflected in a 200–16 vote in the National Constituent Assembly). If that compromise holds, stability will take hold, markets will function, Tunisia will attract investment, and tourism will thrive again.

At the heart of the difference between the two cases is a vision of governance that makes such compromise possible. Such a vision presupposes an assurance that a winner-take-all system will not be established, as well as broad agreement that regulatory institutions should be reasonably nonpartisan and staffed with competent professionals. In the complex global economy of the 21st century, sustained good economic performance requires a panoply of well-functioning institutions that do not fall within a single leader's purview.

China's long-lasting success is sometimes given as a counterexample to the importance of good governance for economic performance. The Chinese example certainly calls into question a strong correlation between multiparty democracy and economic growth.

Democracy is of course something valuable in itself and can be desired independently of its effect on economic growth. But, in the context of economic performance, it is important to emphasize that there is a huge difference between dictatorial regimes, where a single individual monopolizes all power—à la Mubarak or Syrian President Bashar al-Assad—and China, where there has been competition and contestability within a large communist party. And it is the party, operating as a fairly inclusive and meritocratic institution, not an autocratic leader, that has governed in the post-Mao period.

Lack of reasonably independent regulation and competent public administration—or, worse, one-person dictatorships—lead inexorably to economic waste and inefficiency, and eventually to political turmoil. We saw this again in cases like Venezuela, where large oil revenues masked the underlying weakness for a while.

Successful economies require a reasonably independent central bank, and competent bank supervision that does not get dragged into short-term politics. They also need regulatory agencies in sectors such as telecommunications and energy that can pursue policies in accordance with broad goals established by the political process, but with appointees selected according to nonpartisan criteria who then exercise their authority in a way that fosters competition open to all.

When credit decisions, public procurement, construction contracts, and price determination reflect only short-term and purely political goals, good economic performance becomes impossible—even in countries with large natural-resource endowments. In countries with little or no such endowments—where innovation, competitive efficiency, and a focus on production rather than rents is all the more important—the lack of good governance will lead to failure more rapidly.

All of this implies that analyzing the determinants of economic success is a subject not just for economists. Why do some societies achieve the compromises needed to sustain an independent judiciary and a modern regulatory framework—both necessary for an efficient modern economy—while others perpetuate a partisan, winner-take-all approach to governance that weakens public policy and erodes private-sector confidence?

The contrast is starkest in emerging countries, but differences also exist among the advanced economies. Perhaps Germany's ability to reach sociopolitical compromise—again demonstrated by the formation of a right-left coalition after the 2013 elections—has been more fundamental to its recent economic success than the details of the fiscal and structural policies it has pursued to achieve it.

July 21, 2014

THE GREAT INCOME DIVIDE

Thomas Piketty's book, *Capital in the Twenty-First Century*, has captured the world's attention, putting the relationship between capital accumulation and inequality at the center of economic debate. What makes Piketty's argument so special is his insistence on a fundamental trend stemming from the very nature of capitalist growth. It is an argument much in the tradition of the great economists of the 19th and early 20th centuries. In an age of tweets, his bestseller falls just short of a thousand pages.

The book's release follows more than a decade of painstaking research by Piketty and others, including Oxford University's Tony Atkinson. There were minor problems with the treatment of the massive data set, particularly the measurement of capital incomes in the United Kingdom.[43] But the long-term trends identified—a rise in capital owners' share of income and the concentration of "primary income" (before taxes and transfers) at the very top of the distribution in the United States and other major economies—remain unchallenged.

The law of diminishing returns leads one to expect the return on each additional unit of capital to decline. A key to Piketty's results is that in recent decades the return to capital has diminished, if at all, proportionately much less than the rate at which capital has been growing, thereby leading to an increasing share of capital income.

Within the framework of textbook microeconomic theory, this happens when the "elasticity of substitution" in the production function is greater than one: capital can be substituted for labor, imperfectly, but with a small enough decline in the rate of return so that the share of capital increases with greater capital intensity. Larry Summers recently argued that in a dynamic context, the evidence for elasticity of substitution greater than one is weak if one measures the return net of depreciation, because depreciation increases proportionately with the growth of the capital stock.[44]

But traditional elasticity of substitution measures the ease of substitution with a given state of technical knowledge. If there is technical change that saves on labor, the result over time looks similar to what high elasticity of substitution would produce. In fact, just a few months ago, Summers himself proposed a reformulation of the production function that distinguished between traditional capital (K1), which remains, to some degree, a complement to labor (L), and a new kind of capital (K2), which would be a perfect substitute for L.[45]

An increase in K2 would lead to increases in output, the rate of return to K1, and capital's share of total income. At the same time, increasing the amount of "effective labor"— that is, K2 + L—would push wages down. This would be true even if the elasticity of substitution between K1 and aggregate effective labor were less than one.

Until recently not much capital could be classified as K2, with machines that could substitute for labor doing so far from perfectly. But, with the rise of "intelligent" machines and software, K2's share of total capital is growing. Oxford University's Carl Benedikt Frey and Michael Osborne estimate that such machines eventually could perform roughly 47% of existing jobs in the United States.[46]

If that is true, the aggregate share of capital is bound to increase. Given that capital ownership remains concentrated among those with high incomes, the share of income going to the very top of the distribution also will rise. The tendency of these capital owners to save a large proportion of their income—and, in many cases, not to have a large number of children—would augment wealth concentration further.

Other factors could help to augment inequality further. One that has been largely neglected in the debate about Piketty's book is the tendency of the superrich to marry one another—an increasingly common phenomenon as more women join the group of high earners.[47] This, too, causes income concentration to occur faster than it did two or three decades ago, when wealthy men married women less likely to have comparably large incomes. Add to that the modern-scale effects on professional and "superstar" incomes—a result of winner-take-all global markets—and a picture emerges of fundamental forces tending to concentrate primary income at the top.

Without potent policies aimed at counteracting these trends, inequality will almost certainly continue to rise in the coming years. Restoring some balance to the income distribution and encouraging social mobility, while strengthening incentives for innovation and growth, will be among the most important—and formidable—challenges of the 21st century.

August 12, 2014

A GREAT BREAKDOWN?

This month—the centenary of the outbreak of World War I—is an opportune time to reflect on big risks. As Michael Spence recently warned, the international order's widening security deficit, reflecting the weakening of whatever global governance we have, is fast becoming the biggest risk facing the world economy.[48] The same point could have been made a century ago.

On July 30, 1914, Austrian warships bombarded Belgrade, five weeks after the assassination of Archduke Franz Ferdinand in Sarajevo. By mid-August, the world was at war. The armistice that was agreed four years later, after about 20 million people had died, amounted only to an interlude before the horror of World War II.

In the years preceding August 1914, until the assassination of the archduke, the global economy performed relatively well: trade expanded worldwide, financial markets seemed healthy, and the business community shrugged off political problems as either temporary or irrelevant. It was a political breakdown that led to three terrible decades for the world economy.

Markets and economic activity can withstand a great deal of political stress and uncertainty—up to the point that the international order breaks down. Today, for example, the economic mood is rather upbeat. The International Monetary Fund (IMF) forecasts 4% growth for the world economy in 2015,[49] while stock-market indexes are up in many parts of the world; indeed, the Dow-Jones reached an all-time high in July.

In the last few months, however, a civilian airliner was downed in eastern Ukraine by a sophisticated Russian-made missile, tensions have increased around disputed islands in the South and East China Seas, and chaos in the Middle East has continued to spread. The Israeli-Palestinian conflict is in one of its worst phases in decades, with the renewed frustration unleashed by the massive loss of civilian life in Gaza likely to encourage extreme reactions. Terrorists may be on the verge of designing much less detectable weapons.

There are other, less "political" dangers. West Africa is afflicted by a terrible outbreak of the deadly Ebola virus, which will kill thousands of people. The outbreak has so far remained regional, but it serves as a reminder that in an age of air travel by millions, no one is safe from the spread of infectious disease. Containing a disease or a terrorist threat by curtailing international travel or transport would devastate the world economy.

Thinking about August 1914 should remind us that great catastrophes can materialize gradually. Leaders can be "sleepwalkers" who fail to manage risk by, say, establishing institutions that can channel the rival interests and claims that fuel international conflict.[50] Such sleepwalking by policymakers caused the financial meltdown of 2008 as well. Its consequences were not as deadly, though the political effects of mass unemployment and the heightened perception of economic insecurity are still with us.

These examples should spur the world to find ways forward for cooperative action. But the opposite appears to be happening. The United Nations seems more paralyzed than ever. The U.S. Congress still has not approved the IMF reform package agreed in 2010, weakening one of the most important international institutions.[51] Partly because the United States makes capital increases and governance reforms in global financial institutions so difficult, the BRICS countries (Brazil, Russia, India, China, and South Africa) have launched their own development bank, to be based in Shanghai.[52]

Likewise, instead of providing a shining example of supranational cooperation and pooled sovereignty for the 21st century, the European Union remains mired in rather petty disputes. While it still cannot fully agree on the design of its banking union, it is allowing Prime Minister Viktor Orbán of Hungary, a member country, to denigrate the democratic and liberal values on which the EU rests.[53]

The way forward cannot be a return to the past, with its clashing nation-states. The future can be secured only by strong cooperation among all those committed to liberal democracy and the rule of law, with no double standards or excuses, and by patient strengthening of international institutions that embody these values and can translate them into practice.

Whenever a global or regional power acts in a way that contradicts these values, or allies itself closely with those who do, it undermines the international order, which should deliver security and increasing prosperity (and to some degree has). The global economy holds great promise, but it is a promise that can be realized only in an international system based on rules, consent, respect, and a shared sense of justice.

The fact that neither the mayhem in the Middle East nor the crisis in Ukraine seems to touch financial markets should not lull us into complacency. The memory of August 1914 should remind us how the world stumbled into catastrophe. As we know—or should know—from the example of climate change, big risks must be managed, even if the probability of worse-case outcomes is low.

March 9, 2015

PUBLICLY FUNDED INEQUALITY

One of the factors driving the massive rise in global inequality and the concentration of wealth at the very top of the income distribution is the interplay between innovation and global markets. In the hands of a capable entrepreneur, a technological breakthrough can be worth billions of dollars, owing to regulatory protections and the winner-take-all nature of global markets. What is often overlooked, however, is the role that public money plays in creating this modern concentration of private wealth.

As the development economist Dani Rodrik recently pointed out, much of the basic investment in new technologies in the United States has been financed with public funds.[54] The funding can be direct, through institutions like the Defense Department or the National Institutes of Health (NIH), or indirect, via tax breaks, procurement practices, and subsidies to academic labs or research centers.

When a research avenue hits a dead end—as many inevitably do—the public sector bears the cost. For those that yield fruit, however, the situation is often very different. Once a new technology is established, private entrepreneurs, with the help of venture capital, adapt it to global market demand, build temporary or long-term monopoly positions, and thereby capture large profits. The government, which bore the burden of a large part of its development, sees little or no return.

One example, flagged by the economist Jeffrey Sachs, is Sovaldi, a drug used to cure hepatitis C.[55] As Sachs explains, the company that sells it, Gilead Sciences, holds a patent for the treatment that will not expire until 2028. As a result, Gilead can charge monopoly prices: $84,000 for a 12-week course of treatment, far more than the few hundred dollars it costs to produce the drug. Last year, sales of Sovaldi and Harvoni—another drug the company sells for $94,000—amounted to $12.4 billion.

Sachs estimates that the private sector spent less than $500 million on research and development to develop Sovaldi—an amount that Gilead was able to recoup in a few weeks of sales. The NIH and the U.S. Department of Veterans Affairs, however, had heavily funded the start-up that developed the drug and was later acquired by Gilead.

There can be no doubting that the imagination, marketing savvy, and management skills of private entrepreneurs are critical to the successful application of a new technology. And the lower prices, better products, and consumer surplus provided by the commercialization of many innovations clearly provide large societal gains. But one should not overlook the role of government in these successes.

Joint OECD-Eurostat data show that direct government expenditures accounted for 31% of R&D spending in the United States in 2012.[56] Adding indirect expenditures, like tax breaks, would bring this figure to at least 35%. Thanks to such public outlays, a few private players are often making huge returns, which are a major cause of excessive income concentration.

There are several ways to change such a system. Rodrik proposes the creation of public venture capital firms—sovereign wealth funds—that take equity positions in exchange for the intellectual advances created through public financing. Another solution would be to reform the tax code to reduce returns when an individual or firm is cashing in on publicly funded research.

Both solutions face difficulties. Sovereign wealth funds would have to be shielded from partisan politics, perhaps by giving them only nonvoting shares. Raising taxes on the beneficiaries of publicly funded research would be a challenge, given that the link between an original breakthrough and the wealth it created might be hard to quantify. There is also the complication of global capital mobility and tax avoidance, which the G-20 is only beginning to address.[57]

Other approaches are also possible: tightening up patent laws or imposing price controls for monopolistic industries, such as pharmaceuticals, as many market economies have done. What would not be a solution, however, would be to channel fewer public resources into research and innovation—key drivers of economic growth.

It does not take huge rates of return to mobilize a lot of talent; something like a 50% profit margin for a few years would be an acceptable reward for particularly good entrepreneurship. Multiples of that amount, however, simply end up as gifts by the public to a few individuals. A combination of measures and international agreements must be found that would allow taxpayers to obtain decent returns on their investments, without removing the incentives for savvy entrepreneurs to commercialize innovative products.

The seriousness of this problem should not be understated. The amounts involved contribute to the creation of a new aristocracy that can pass on its wealth through inheritance. If huge sums can be spent to protect privilege by financing election campaigns (as is now the case in the United States), the implications of this problem, for both democracy and long-term economic efficiency, could become systemic. The possible solutions are far from simple, but they are well worth seeking.

May 13, 2015

THE PARADOX OF IDENTITY POLITICS

The United Kingdom's recent general election provided a clear example of how the question of national identity is reshaping Europe's political landscape. The Scottish National Party, embodying a left-wing version of identity politics, wiped out Labour in Scotland, allowing the Conservatives to gain an absolute majority in parliament. The government of Prime Minister David Cameron—who has focused on British identity, rather than the UK's common destiny with Europe—will undoubtedly hold a referendum on the UK's continued membership in the European Union, with unpredictable consequences.

For decades, political debate in Europe focused largely on economic institutions and policies. Conservatives argued for a private sector–driven economy, unfettered markets, low taxes, reduced government spending, and limited public goods. Liberals and Social Democrats supported a private-ownership economy, markets, European integration, and increased trade, tempered by substantially redistributive taxes and transfers, a strong social safety net, and some public ownership in areas such as infrastructure and finance.

In this bipolar system, the parties differed on the nuances of economic policy, but broadly agreed on democratic values, the European project, and the need to adapt to and manage globalization, rather than reject it wholesale. But, with the growing success of appeals to identity and renewed ethnic or religious nationalism, that is changing. Are the ghosts of the early and mid-20th century returning?

The question is particularly relevant for Europe, but it also has global significance. In the Middle East, for example, identity politics is manifesting itself in its most sinister form: a chaotic and violent clash between Sunni and Shia Muslims, exemplified by the rise of the Islamic State.

Loyalty to a perceived identity can have innocuous and enriching components, such as, say, the promotion of a regional language. The problem with identity politics is that it places the "in" group at odds with the perceived "other"—an approach that can easily foster chauvinism, invidious discrimination, and open antagonism.

One major reason for the resurgence of identity politics in Europe is globalization, which has limited the capacity of countries or peoples to control their economies. Indeed, the global economy has become so interconnected, and world markets so powerful, that there appears to be little scope for national policies to disrupt hyper-mobile capital flows.

While globalization has helped to boost overall prosperity, it has been most beneficial for those who form the new global elite. Meanwhile, many people in Europe face greater economic insecurity, owing to new technologies or competition from lower-cost workers elsewhere. Unless they can upgrade their knowledge and skills—and, in some cases, move to a new industry or location—they face constrained economic opportunities. These disadvantaged groups are particularly large in the countries that were hit hardest by the recent global financial crisis and now struggle with high unemployment.

But even people who are relatively prosperous are frustrated by some features of globalization. They may oppose the use of their taxes to "subsidize" poorer people who do not share their identity, such as immigrants, French-speaking Belgians, southern Italians, or Greeks.

When it comes to trade protectionism, European integration, and economic globalization, those on the far right and the far left often share the same views. In France, for example, many supporters of the National Front voted communist 30 years ago. And, indeed, the National Front's economic program is rather similar to that of the Left Front (an electoral bloc comprising the French Communist Party and the Left Party).

Of course, when it comes to immigration and human rights, the internationalist ideological tradition of socialism prevents extreme nationalist and racist discourse on the far left. But, given that these parties are competing with the far right for the same disenchanted voters, their humanism on these issues has become a severe political handicap, which may explain why the extreme right has lately been more successful electorally.

Meanwhile, the rise of identity-driven political movements presents a huge challenge for Europe's traditional political parties.[58] Mainstream conservatives, widely perceived as being in thrall to the economic interests of the wealthy, must find ways to appear populist—but without sounding too much like their far-right competitors on immigration and human rights. Cameron has succeeded in this delicate balancing act—and has been rewarded by voters. Mainstream Republicans in the United States, pressured by the more extreme forces within their party, face a similar challenge.

For center-left parties, the task is even more daunting. They must offer voters a realistic economic program that is market friendly and open to international trade, while promising tangible benefits to the poorer 60–70% of the population who are understandably frustrated with their lack of economic progress. If a left party's economic policy is perceived as a weak copy of the right's agenda, the poorest segments of the population will gravitate to chauvinist forces and their false promises of protection from the consequences of globalization.

The upcoming elections in Spain, Turkey, Denmark, and Portugal—not to mention next year's U.S. presidential election—will present their own versions of these challenges. The left, in particular, will have to defend the principles of equality and democracy, while finding ways to manage irreversible globalization, including through international cooperation. The great paradox is that if the rise of identity politics continues, governments will be even less able to address the problems that are fueling it.

June 10, 2015

A NEW BIRTH FOR SOCIAL DEMOCRACY?

Nowadays, with the global economy undergoing fundamental transformation, workers worldwide are coming under significant pressure. Particularly in developed economies, social policies must adjust to provide the support that lower-income groups need, while encouraging growth and advancing well-being.

The pressure has been unrelenting and inescapable. In the United States, real (inflation-adjusted) compensation for men with only a high school diploma fell by 21% from 1979 to 2013.[59] In much of Europe, which provides stronger wage protection, unemployment has soared, especially since the euro crisis began in 2008. Germany and some Northern European countries remain an exception, although the German labor market contains a large low-wage, mini-jobs segment.

Driving these trends is the changing nature of work. For starters, services have been gaining ground worldwide, especially in developed economies. From 1970 to 2012, the GDP share of services in the Organization for Economic

Cooperation and Development countries increased from 53% to 71%.

New technology and "intelligent" machines are not only displacing many types of workers in both the manufacturing and services sectors, they are also facilitating the rise of new business models, in which individuals perform (mostly low-paid service) jobs within loose networks, instead of as dedicated employees of structured organizations. For example, the ride-sharing service Uber now has 162,000 active drivers in the U.S. alone and is displacing traditional taxi services.[60] The startup Handy hopes that its app achieves similar success in connecting customers to independent contractors providing various household services. As technology races ahead and value chains become globalized, workers must adapt, whether by changing jobs, relocating, or acquiring new skills—a challenge that is particularly burdensome for older workers, but demands a new approach to life planning for all.

Some people—especially those who acquired valued and flexible skills early in life, as well as those who are already in strong positions because of inherited wealth—can flourish in this new economy. Millions of others, however, are ill-prepared for the new age. And it is their growing anxiety that is fueling the rise of identity politics, with populist leaders and movements appealing to ethnic or religious solidarity in the face of the impersonal forces of change.[61]

Center-left parties face a particularly difficult challenge, as their lower-income electoral base is lured away by anti-immigration, chauvinist competitors. Making matters worse, the fragmentation of production (whether in goods or services), together with intensifying fiscal pressures, militates against these parties' traditional reliance on collective bargaining to create systems and policies that ensure citizens against shocks and misfortune.

The right-wing response to this challenge—essentially to dismantle the welfare state—would leave the majority of citizens exposed to economic shocks and structural shifts (merely reinforcing their sense of isolation and vulnerability). The progressive response, by contrast, must entail strong social policies—including both insurance and protection—compatible with new technologies and types of work. Concretely, this means that instead of generalized social protection, each citizen would have a lifelong individual budget of support and security, while requiring that eligible recipients show initiative in determining how to adapt.

The main difference between the progressive vision of a society underpinned by these "citizen accounts" and the conservative idea that individual citizens should create personal retirement accounts, take out student loans, or cover their own health insurance is the public sector's role. Not only would the public sector take primary responsibility for financing social protection, public policy would also frame cooperation among government, employers, and recipients to eliminate duplication and bolster effectiveness and fairness.

For example, a lifelong "family account" would enable paid maternity and paternity leave, provide child-care support, and allow time away from work to care for the sick or elderly. It would combine some general rules with income-adjusted financial contributions by the state, employers, and individuals. A "learning account" would set the parameters for educational support, including lifelong opportunities to acquire new skills and to teach skills to others.

Basic forms of such a scheme already exist in many countries. Norway offers 49 weeks of parental leave with full pay to a couple of parents, or 58 weeks with 80% pay. Both parents must use at least 10% of their budget, but they can also roll part of it over to use when their children start school (and again benefit greatly from parental support). Of course, few countries are as wealthy as Norway; but the principle—including support for elder care—can be applied to 30-, 40-, or 50-week periods. France, too, is now moving in this direction, creating "individual activity accounts" that aim to streamline its social policies, without sacrificing its sense of national solidarity.

To be sure, this approach will not magically resolve all of the challenges countries currently face. Fiscal constraints will remain, as governments continue to fund public goods. Adequate taxation of high-income individuals and high-profit companies, together with strong and sustained efforts to reduce tax avoidance, will become even more vital to defend the revenue base. And unions will still be needed to defend their members' interests.

Nonetheless, a new social contract is needed to account for the increasingly important role that individual preferences, and individual responsibility, play in today's world. Each citizen should feel empowered, not isolated and abandoned, in the face of globalization and technological transformation.

With this approach, social democracy can again drive progress, instead of being stifled by identity politics and market fundamentalism. That would serve not only the cause of social justice, but also the goal of sustaining the skilled, happy, and healthy workforce that a successful economy requires.[62]

December 17, 2015

RESTORING YESTERDAY'S HOPE FOR TOMORROW'S WORLD

The year 2015 was difficult, punctuated by declining growth forecasts, horrific terror attacks, massive refugee flows, and serious political challenges, with populism on the rise in many countries. In the Middle East, in particular, chaos and violence have continued to proliferate, with devastating consequences. This represents a disappointing turn from the undoubtedly flawed, but far more hopeful, world of just a few decades ago.

In his autobiography, *The World of Yesterday*, Stefan Zweig described a similarly drastic change.[63] Born in 1881 in Vienna, Zweig spent his youth in an optimistic, civil, and tolerant environment. Then, starting in 1914, he witnessed Europe's collapse into World War I, followed by revolutionary convulsions, the Great Depression, the rise of Stalinism, and finally the barbarism of Nazism and the outbreak of World War II. Devastated, Zweig committed suicide while in exile in 1942.

One imagines that Zweig would have been comforted by the post-WWII creation of the United Nations and the

Bretton-Woods system, not to mention the subsequent decades of reconstruction and reconciliation. He could have witnessed the cooperation and progress that marked the postwar era. Perhaps, then, he would have looked at the period from 1914 to 1945 as a terrible but limited detour in the world's march toward peace and prosperity.

Of course, the second half of the twentieth century was far from perfect. Until 1990, peace was secured largely by the threat of mutual nuclear destruction. Local conflicts, such as in Korea, Vietnam, parts of Africa, and the Middle East, took their toll. And while about 100 developing countries gained independence, the process was not always peaceful.

At the same time, however, the world economy grew more rapidly than ever. A strong middle class emerged in the advanced countries, and then began to appear elsewhere. The Western democracies and Japan built economies in which productivity growth led to shared prosperity; governments engaged in regulation and redistribution, while private companies fueled growth by implementing technologically advanced production methods.

On both the regional and global levels, decisive progress was made in reaping the benefits from trade and economies of scale. The European integration project seemed to herald a new kind of cooperation, which could extend to other regions and even influence global cooperation.

The generation that came of age in the 1960s, which includes myself, felt much like Zweig had felt in his youth. We believed that, though progress may not be linear, we could count on it. We expected an increasingly peaceful and tolerant world, in which technological advances, together with well-governed markets, would generate ever-expanding prosperity. In 1989, when the Soviet Union was poised to collapse and China was shifting to a market-based economy, Francis Fukuyama announced the "end of history."[64]

Over the last two decades, however, our hopes—political, social, and economic—have been repeatedly dashed. There was a time when U.S. policymakers were wondering whether Russia should join NATO. That possibility is difficult even to consider today, after Russia's intervention in Ukraine and annexation of Crimea (apparently carried out in response to fears that Ukraine would deepen its ties with the European Union and NATO).

Many emerging economies achieved rapid growth for years—even decades—enabling billions of people to escape extreme poverty and reducing the wealth gap between developed and developing countries. But that growth has lately slowed substantially, leading many to question whether economists spoke too soon when we labeled them the new engines of global economic growth.[65]

Likewise, the Arab Spring in 2011 was supposed to herald a new, more democratic future for the Middle East and North Africa. While Tunisia has averted disaster, most of the other affected countries have ended up mired in chaos, with Syria's brutal civil war facilitating the rise of the Islamic State.

The euro, meanwhile, suffered its own crisis. The common currency, once portrayed as the start of a quasi-federal Europe, instead created serious tension between "creditor" and "debtor" countries when many debtors faced a protracted economic downturn. Just as Europe seemed finally to be escaping the euro crisis, refugees, especially from Syria, began flooding in. That has jeopardized the Schengen area of borderless travel, and some are asking whether the EU can withstand the pressure.

In the United States, the Syrian refugee crisis has led Congress to rush to restrict visa-free entrance for tourists from 38 countries. This comes at a time when income and wealth inequality is skyrocketing in the United States—the median wage for men has not increased in decades—leaving many to wonder whether their children will be able to maintain the living standard they enjoyed. On top of all this, for the first time in decades, the growth of international trade no longer comfortably exceeds the growth of global output.

A fundamental driver of many of these problems may well be the unprecedented speed of change—driven by globalization and technological innovation—which has produced disruptions too quickly and on too large a scale to manage. For example, while communication technology has done wonders, say, to expand access to finance in Africa, it has also enabled terrorist networks to encrypt their communications effectively. And as the global financial crisis starkly demonstrated, regulators have struggled to keep pace with financial innovation.

The potential for human progress still seems immense, because the world wants for neither resources nor technological innovation. Indeed, technology offers the hope of lifesaving medical treatments, higher economic productivity, and sustainable energy systems. But people are fearful, as shown by the return of identity politics and a lack of economic and political inclusiveness. As a result, productivity growth is slowing, and, though capital seems cheap and profits plentiful, investment remains sluggish.

The key to managing the disruptions and assuaging people's fears is governance. Zweig saw the world fall apart a century ago not because human knowledge stopped advancing, but because of widespread governance and policy failures. As we enter 2016, we must focus on adapting governance, in all of its economic and political dimensions, to the 21st century, so that our resources and knowledge produce inclusive progress, not violent conflict.

PART III

EUROPE: BEYOND CRISIS MANAGEMENT

The Greek financial crisis burst into the open in the fall of 2009, after George Papandreou's newly elected government had to announce that the actual fiscal deficit was much larger than what had been communicated to the European Commission by the former government. The Irish crisis followed a year later in October 2010. The causes of the two "trigger crises" were very different, the first a massive public finance problem made worse by prior manipulation of the official statistics, the second a banking crisis in a country with sound public finances.

Spain, Portugal, and Italy followed Greece and Ireland in losing the confidence of the markets: Spain resembled Ireland in that what triggered the crisis was the bursting of a huge real estate bubble and the ensuing banking crisis; Portugal and Italy were milder cases of a Greece-like budget problem. These differences notwithstanding, all five of these "periphery" countries saw their sovereign borrowing costs soar to entirely unsustainable levels at the end of 2010 and in 2011. The Irish and Spanish banking crises turned into sovereign debt crises, similar to those of Greece and Portugal, as governments were forced to rescue their national banking systems. Italy never had a full-fledged crisis, but its sovereign yields rose to levels not far from those of the other periphery countries. In all these cases the decline in the value of sovereign bonds in turn weakened the capital adequacy positions of the banking systems, because of the high share of their countries' "national" sovereign bonds on the balance sheets of financial institutions. The sovereign debt and banking problems became inextricably linked.

The essays in this third section are both a chronicle of the Eurozone crisis and reflections on the future of Europe against the backdrop of the technological, social, and governance issues discussed in the essays of parts I and II. During the period these essays were written it was the Eurozone crisis that was the major challenge for Europe. From mid-2015 onward, however, the refugee crisis became a new and dominant challenge. In the summer of 2015, an unexpectedly large influx of refugees and other migrants had started pouring into Europe, threatening the Schengen area arrangements. By spring 2016, the flow of refugees into Germany had slowed down markedly, although the number reaching Italy from Africa seemed to increase again.

While the refugee crisis has very different dimensions from the Eurozone crisis, both have undermined Europe's progress by exposing serious erosion in the sense of common destiny and solidarity on which the whole European project was built. This was even more obvious in connection with the refugee crisis: when Italy and Greece had asked for burden sharing as they began to deal with large numbers of refugees landing on their shores, they were essentially told it was their problem to handle; but when in mid-2015 the surge was into Germany, it was all of a sudden Germany that asked for burden sharing. True, many Germans would argue that the problems in the South were caused by the countries themselves, whereas the refugee surge was an "external shock" for Germany. But this is only partially so. Both the world financial crisis and the contagion effects inside the Eurozone itself were also "external shocks" to many of the countries that faced difficulties, such as Spain.

The European Union, and Europe as a whole, is indeed at a crossroads. In the coming two or three years Europe will either be able to redesign and reenergize itself, or it will suffer from increased dislocation and may slowly become irrelevant. Contrary to what appears common wisdom among many European leaders, Europe really can no longer "muddle through," but needs a systemic transformation to regain the support of citizens and deliver on what remains a huge promise of postnational governance.

Four themes run through the "European" essays. First, the financial crisis in Europe displayed many elements of a more global governance crisis. Why is it so difficult to coordinate macroeconomic policies in order to reduce macro-imbalances and produce more growth for all? The northern part of the Eurozone has all along been running a huge current account surplus, incompatible with desirable macroeconomic balances both from a European and global perspective. The periphery countries have been forced to reduce their current account deficits, without the northern countries reducing their surpluses. As a result, as these lines are written, the Eurozone taken as a whole is running a large surplus. When one adds the non-Eurozone countries of Switzerland, Sweden, Denmark, and Norway to the Eurozone group, the "Northern European" current account surplus becomes huge, close to half a trillion US$, larger than China's ever was.

These macroeconomic imbalances are of course closely linked to the degree of fiscal austerity that has been pursued and suggest that fiscal retrenchment has been excessive, at least in countries such as Germany that have had ongoing current-account surpluses. For technology and global competitiveness–related issues, Europe needs both deep supply-side structural reforms as well as a new social contract. But excessive austerity, far from having helped, made these reforms very difficult to agree on. This is the second major theme addressed in part III. More rapid structural reforms, greater macroeconomic policy coordination, and an appropriate degree of medium-term fiscal policy discipline form a policy package that can only work well if it is indeed a package. Often economics is like medicine: remedies work as a package, but can actually be harmful if administered in isolation. Bold structural reforms need both a sense of shared challenge and willingness to incur some upfront costs, but also fiscal space and financing as well as social solidarity measures that allow the patient to breathe while the restructuring takes place.

The third and fourth themes focus on the implications of these needs for macroeconomic coordination and for new social policy design. Three essays emphasize the special role of Germany, France, and their relationship. Germany and France have been the historical "motor" making the European integration project feasible. I argue that this partnership remains absolutely essential for Europe, and, in particular, for governance in the Eurozone. One of these essays draws attention to the crucial role France plays in linking northern to southern Europe. France, alone, is both northern and southern. Germany is the current powerhouse of Europe, but France, in a very specific way, makes Europe possible.

The United Kingdom, too, is critical to the European project. Europe could survive without the United Kingdom—it could not without either France or Germany— but it would be a Europe much diminished in scale and global power, both hard and soft. In order to keep the United Kingdom in Europe and at the same time move forward with the desirable further fiscal-political integration in the Eurozone, I have long argued that what was needed is "Two Europes in One." One of the essays details this vision in terms of the institutional reforms required. At the time of writing, the United Kingdom has not yet held its June referendum on the "Brexit." Indeed while a language of compromise with respect to the UK's demands was agreed at the February 19 European Summit, the full details of the institutional change proposals that language points to are very complex. They have not been as simple and as radical as what I proposed in the "Two Europes in One" article. Nonetheless, they did recognize that the European Union is in a permanent way a multicurrency area containing a currency union. That recognition is a key necessity as argued in part of my essay. The need for much more of a "concentric circles" institutional architecture than was envisioned when the Treaty of Lisbon was finalized, about a decade ago, has become stronger, all through the discussions surrounding both the Eurozone crisis as well as the British referendum.

As argued in many of the essays in all parts of this collection—if the world is to successfully manage the great disruptions lying ahead, governance in the 21st century must, at the same time, be more multilevel, more local, and more global than it ever has been. Europe's success, in a renewed form, remains as critical, if not more so, than it was right after 1945, for peace, democracy, and a better globalization worldwide.

Postscript: As this book was going to press, voters in the United Kingdom voted on the Brexit referendum to take the UK out of the European Union. The vote, on June 23, 2016, stunned the world. It underlines the deep disagreements about what constitutes progress to which many of these essays refer. The Brexit vote quickly became a huge new source of political and economic uncertainty, and it will take months to become clearer what kind of Europe it may lead to.

THE GLOBAL FUTURE OF EUROPE'S CRISIS

It is now clear that the Eurozone crisis will continue well into 2012, despite early February's recovery in stock markets. Negotiations between Greece and the banks over Greek sovereign debt may yet be concluded, but sufficiently wide participation by banks in the deal remains very much in doubt. Meanwhile, the International Monetary Fund (IMF) has raised the issue of official-sector debt reduction, possibly even by the European Central Bank (ECB), sending the message that a "haircut" for private bondholders will not be enough to return Greece to financial sustainability.

The IMF's concerns are valid, but its idea is being resisted fiercely, owing to fears of political contagion: other debt-distressed Eurozone countries might press for equal treatment. Moreover, the promised increase in IMF resources that would allow it to build a stronger firewall against financial contagion has still not arrived. And all of the changes agreed upon for the European Stabilization Fund and the European Stability Mechanism have yet to be implemented.

Of course, some positive steps have been taken. The ECB's generous provision of liquidity to European banks at only 1% interest for up to three years has prevented a banking crisis from piling on top of the sovereign debt crisis. But that initiative has not succeeded in reducing the "problem" countries' longer-term borrowing costs to levels compatible with their projected growth rates: there is just too much long-term uncertainty, and growth prospects are simply too discouraging. Indeed, in mid-January Standard & Poor's downgraded AAA-rated France and Austria, in addition to seven other Eurozone countries—Slovenia, Slovakia, Spain, Malta, Italy, Cyprus, and Portugal.

It now seems clear to almost everyone that one key challenge facing the Eurozone stems from the fact that it is a monetary union without being an economic union, an arrangement that has no counterpart anywhere. As a result, divergences in production costs over time cannot be compensated for by exchange-rate adjustments.

In the absence of somewhat higher inflation in the surplus countries, say, 4% a year, adjustment requires deflation in the crisis countries to bring about a noticeable relative decline in production costs over time. In practice, such deflation can be achieved only at the cost of high unemployment and social distress. It is therefore unclear whether the current strategy of combining austerity and deflation is politically feasible, which explains the huge uncertainty hanging over the entire Eurozone.

Somewhat higher inflation in the surplus countries and larger cross-border resource transfers would give the deficit countries more time, allowing for structural reforms to produce results and reducing the need for deflation. But northern European surplus countries reject such an approach, fearing that it would weaken the pressure on southern European debtor countries to undertake structural reforms in the first place.

Beyond the specific problems of the monetary union, there is also a global dimension to Europe's challenges—the tension, emphasized by authors such as Dani Rodrik, and Jean Michel Severino and Olivier Ray—between national democratic politics and globalization. Trade, communication, and financial linkages have created a degree of interdependence among national economies, which, together with heightened vulnerability to financial-market swings, has restricted national policymakers' freedom of action everywhere.

Perhaps the most dramatic sign of this tension came when Greece's then prime minister, George Papandreou, announced a referendum on the policy package proposed to allow Greece to stay in the Eurozone. While one can debate the merits of referenda for decisionmaking, the heart of the problem was the very notion of holding a national debate for several weeks, given that markets move in hours or minutes. It took less than 24 hours for Papandreou's proposal to collapse under the pressure of financial markets (and European leaders' fear of them).

Around the world, the stock of financial assets has become so large, relative to national income flows, that financial-market movements can overwhelm most countries. Even the largest economies are vulnerable, particularly if they are highly dependent on debt finance. If, for some reason, financial markets or China's central bank, or both, were suddenly to reject U.S. Treasury bonds, interest rates would soar, sending the American economy into recession.

But being a creditor does not provide strong protection, either. If Americans' appetite for Chinese exports suddenly collapsed because of a financial panic in the United

States, China itself would find itself in serious economic trouble.

These interlinked threats are real, and they require much stronger global economic policy cooperation. Citizens, however, want to understand what is going on, debate policies, and give their consent to the types of cooperation proposed. Thus, a more supranational form of politics is needed to re-embed markets in democratic processes, as happened during the course of the 20th century with national politics and national markets.

The scale of this challenge becomes apparent when one sees how difficult it is to coordinate economic policies even in the European Union, which has moved much further than any other group of countries in the direction of supranational cooperation. Nonetheless, unless globalization can be slowed down or partly reversed, which is unlikely and undesirable in the long run, the kind of "politics beyond borders" for which Europe is groping will become a global necessity.

Indeed, the European crisis may be providing a mere foretaste of what will likely be the central political debate of the first half of the 21st century: how to resolve the tension between global markets and national politics.

May 14, 2012

REBALANCING THE EUROZONE

The Eurozone crisis unfolded primarily as a sovereign debt crisis mostly on its southern periphery, with interest rates on sovereign bonds at times reaching 6–7% for Italy and Spain, and even higher for other countries. And, because Eurozone banks hold a substantial part of their assets in the form of Eurozone sovereign bonds, the sovereign debt crisis became a potential banking crisis, worsened by banks' other losses, owing, for example, to the collapse of housing prices in Spain. So a key challenge in resolving the Eurozone crisis is to reduce the southern countries' debt burdens.

The change in a country's debt burden reflects the size of its primary budget balance (the balance minus interest payments) as a share of GDP, as well as the difference between its borrowing costs and its GDP growth rate. When the difference between borrowing costs and growth becomes too large, the primary budget surpluses required to stop debt from increasing become impossible to achieve. Indeed, growth in southern Europe is expected to be close to zero or negative for the next two years, and is not expected to exceed 2–3% even in the longer term.

While not always evident from the headlines, an underlying cause of the Eurozone crisis—and now an obstacle for growth in the south—has been the divergence in production costs that developed between the peripheral countries, notably the "south" (specifically, Greece, Spain, Italy, and Portugal) and the "north" (for simplicity, Germany) during the first decade after the introduction of the euro. Unit labor costs in the four southern countries increased by 36%, 28%, 30%, and 25%, respectively, from 2000 to 2010, compared to less than 5% in Germany, resulting in an end-2010 cumulative divergence above 30% in Greece and more than 20% in Portugal, Italy, and Spain.

Unit labor costs reflect compensation levels and productivity: gains in productivity can offset the effect of wage growth. Productivity performance did not vary dramatically between northern and southern European countries from 2000 to 2010—in fact, average annual productivity growth was faster in Greece than in Germany (1% versus 0.7%). But labor costs increased much faster in the south, resulting in differential cost increases that cannot be addressed by devaluation as long as the monetary union endures.

As long as this internal divergence persists, the euro crisis cannot be fully resolved, because current-account deficits or slow growth, or both, will continue to stalk the southern European countries, perpetuating worries about sovereign debt and commercial banks.

In this context, productivity growth—whether through technical progress, better allocation of resources, or productive investment—is as important a variable for the southern economies as wage restraint is. Indeed, excessive wage deflation is likely to have negative effects on productivity. Skilled labor is likely to emigrate faster, and extreme austerity, falling prices, and high unemployment—and the resulting likelihood of social tension—are not exactly conducive to investment, innovation, or labor mobility.

Likewise, while reducing employment is one way to boost productivity, it implies high macroeconomic costs in terms of lost revenues and higher social spending. Perhaps even more important, economic policy should not break a society's confidence in itself; what economists call "animal spirits" must be able to reflect hope for the future.

For all of these reasons, excessive austerity and deflation could make the "reforms" to improve the southern European countries' competitiveness impossible to implement. The right approach must combine reasonable wage restraint and low (but not negative) inflation with microeconomic policy measures aimed at encouraging productivity increases.

Moreover, it is clear that northern European countries could help to close the competitiveness gap more rapidly by encouraging faster wage growth. Indeed, Western policymakers' strong focus on persuading the Chinese authorities to permit greater appreciation of their currency is puzzling when one considers that Germany's current-account surplus, as a share of GDP, is now much larger than China's.

Reversing the large differential in unit labor costs that has emerged in the euro's first decade thus requires not only wage restraint and productivity-enhancing reforms in the south, but also higher wage gains in the north. A simulation shows that if German wages grew at 4% annually instead of the 1.5% of the last decade, and if annual productivity growth in Spain accelerated to 2% (it was close to 0.7% in both countries), Spain could in five years reverse the unit-labor-cost differential with Germany that has emerged since 2000, with Spanish wages growing at about 1.7% per annum.

This should not be an impossible scenario. It would

require restraint in Spain, where wages grew at an average annual rate of 3.4% in 2000–10, as well as a serious effort to accelerate productivity growth. But it would not require falling wages or significant price deflation: annual wage growth of 1.7% and productivity growth of 2% would be compatible with inflation close to zero. Productivity growth at the historical rate of 0.7% in Germany, with wage growth of 4%, would be compatible with an inflation rate a little above 3%.

In short, internal adjustment in the Eurozone is achievable without serious deflation in the south, provided that productivity growth there accelerates, and that the north does its part by encouraging modestly faster wage gains. The smaller current-account surplus in northern Europe that might result from this should itself be welcome. If the north insists on maintaining the low wage growth of the 2000–10 period, internal adjustment would require significant unemployment and deflation in the south, making it more difficult and perhaps politically impossible to achieve.

August 1, 2012

MARIO DRAGHI'S GUNS OF AUGUST

August has been a dangerous month in European history, but this year it could be the turning point for the Eurozone—and perhaps for the world economy. On July 26, Mario Draghi, president of the European Central Bank (ECB), declared that his institution would do "whatever it takes" to preserve the euro, and added: "Believe me, it will be enough."

Draghi's strong—indeed, unprecedented—statement was widely interpreted as signaling that the ECB would soon revive its bond-purchase program, focusing on Spanish debt in particular. Stock markets around the world soared. Jens Weidemann of the Bundesbank immediately expressed reservations, but the next day German Chancellor Angela Merkel and French President François Hollande issued a joint statement expressing their determination "to do everything in order to protect the Eurozone."

I recently argued that the ECB, working with the nascent European Stability Mechanism (ESM), was the only institution that could save the Eurozone.[66] It could do so by buying Italian and Spanish bonds in the secondary market with the pre-announced intention of keeping their sovereign interest rates below a certain threshold for a certain time.

It is likely that Draghi's statement will indeed be followed by ECB purchases of Spanish (and Italian) sovereign bonds. A man like Draghi would not have issued such a statement without believing that he could follow through on it. But, if this is to become a decisive turning point in the Eurozone crisis, three things must happen.

First, the ECB's renewed bond purchases must express the clear intention of reducing sovereign interest rates to sustainable levels, which are at least 200 basis points below their July averages. A high-level German diplomat reportedly dismissed Spain's 6.5–7% interest rates recently, on the grounds that Spain borrowed at nearly the same rates in the 1990s. But that statement, amazingly, ignored

Spain's higher pre-euro inflation—thus confusing real and nominal rates—and more rapid GDP growth.

For countries that are following agreed reform programs, the ECB should commit itself to bringing down interest rates to levels compatible with projected inflation and growth rates, and announce how long (say, nine months) this will continue. A sporadic program without such announced objectives is unlikely to work, and could even be counterproductive, as private investors might well demand even higher returns because the growing ECB share of the debt would be considered senior, augmenting their risk.

That would not happen if the ECB announced—and demonstrated—its determination to bring down interest rates, whatever it takes, for a significant period of time. Doing so would allow the Eurozone to establish the institutional and legal means to achieve greater cooperation and integration, as agreed at the European Council's meeting in June.

The second thing that must happen is that Eurozone leaders and parliaments, with the cooperation of the courts, must be seen to push ahead with institutional reforms to establish not only the ESM, but also a banking union and partial debt mutualization. But, while greater merging of economic sovereignty is the only long-term solution to the Eurozone's woes, such reforms cannot happen very quickly, which is why the ECB's role is so crucial. The Eurozone can no longer sustain continued uncertainty and high real interest rates in the peripheral countries, so the ECB must provide a solid and credible bridge to the future.

Finally, the adjustment programs themselves must be

carefully recalibrated. It should be clear by now that excessive, front-loaded austerity measures tend to be self-defeating, because they trigger a downward spiral of output, employment, and tax revenues. Indeed, the International Monetary Fund's most recent report on the Eurozone says as much (if cautiously).[67]

The pace of deficit reduction must be slowed, particularly in Spain, because output is determined in the short run by demand, and private demand cannot replace public demand until a degree of faith in the future is restored. This move toward support of effective demand must be combined with the kind of structural reforms that will allow more rapid, supply-side growth in the longer term.

If these three steps—an ECB bond-buying program to hold down sovereign interest rates, concrete progress on establishing a real economic union, and realistic revision of current adjustment programs—could be achieved as a package, the resources that the ECB would need to use for its bond purchases would drop, because credibility would be restored. Even if there is further bad news for Europe—from Greece, for example, or from a sharper-than-expected slowdown in China—the Eurozone could begin to move out of crisis mode this month.

But that is possible only if, this time, the "big bazooka" really is put in place. Otherwise, the Eurozone's position—financially, politically, and socially—will soon become indefensible.

September 12, 2012

EUROPE'S VITAL FRENCH CONNECTION

In the debates raging over the future of the European Union and the Eurozone, Germany always takes center stage. It has the largest economy, accounting for 28% of Eurozone GDP and 25% of the Eurozone's population. It is running a current-account surplus that is now larger than China's—indeed, the largest in the world in absolute value. And, while weighted majorities can overrule it on some issues, everyone acknowledges that little can be done in the Eurozone unless Germany agrees.

But the emphasis on Germany, though justified, should not lead to an underestimation of France's critical role. France not only accounts for roughly 22% of Eurozone GDP and 20% of its population—behind only Germany—but also has the healthiest demography in the Eurozone, whereas the German population is projected to decline over the next decade.

At the same time, France's critical role reflects more than its size. Indeed, in terms of influencing outcomes in Europe, France is as important as Germany, for three reasons.

First, France is an indispensable link between southern and northern Europe at a time of growing economic and financial division between creditors and debtors (a fissure that has begun to assume a cultural dimension). An active France can play a bridging role, leveraging its strong relationship with Germany (a friendship that is a pillar of the EU) and its proximity and cultural affinities to the Mediterranean.

France is "southern" in its current-account deficit, but "northern" in its borrowing costs (slightly above Germany's), owing partly to inflows of capital fleeing the south, as well as to modest but positive economic growth. Moreover, there is no perceived "re-denomination" risk affecting French assets, given markets' confidence that France will retain the euro. So, while France faces huge economic challenges, its northern and southern features permit it to play a proactive role in the European project's survival.

French President François Hollande has already given a rather successful preview of this role, meeting German Chancellor Angela Merkel in Berlin on his first day in office, and, a month later, participating in a high-profile meeting with the Italian and Spanish prime ministers in Rome. Indeed, he took the lead in adding a "growth pact" to the "stability pact" that had been negotiated under Merkel's leadership.

Second, France, under its new center-left government, must demonstrate that the "European model" of a market economy coupled with strong social solidarity can be reformed and strengthened, rather than abandoned—not just in Europe's more pragmatic north, but also in its more ideological south. French Socialists will not renounce their traditional commitments; nor should they. But they now have the opportunity to contribute to the European model's renewal.

Under Hollande, France's Socialists favor achieving that renewal through a process of social dialogue that convinces rather than imposes, that focuses both on revenue measures and on boosting government efficiency, and that may adopt some of northern Europe's more successful "flexicurity" policies, which combine greater labor-market flexibility with strong social protection. The reforms should also introduce much greater individual choice, permitting solutions to retirement, education, health, and lifestyle issues that can be more easily tailored to citizens' specific circumstances and needs.

The government of Hollande and Prime Minister Jean-Marc Ayrault has strong majorities at all executive and legislative levels, giving it a rare opportunity to act. If it can renew the European model at home, it will be able to project that success much more widely, particularly in southern Europe, in turn reinforcing confidence and belief in the EU, particularly among the young generation. The French center-left must lead in conceiving a vision for Europe in which solidarity and equity reinforce long-term economic strength.

Finally, along with the United Kingdom among European countries, France retains more of a global role than Germany has yet acquired. While the United Nations Security Council is outdated in its structure, it still plays a crucial legitimizing role; and France, not Germany, is a member. In many other international organizations as well, France punches above its weight.

Similarly, while France exports much less than Germany outside the EU, many large French enterprises rival Germany's in global reach and technical know-how. And French is still a global language. In other words, France not only is a link between Europe's north and south, but also contributes substantially to linking Europe to the rest of the world.

Europe needs a renewed vision and effective policies to realize that vision. France's Socialist-Green government can play a critical unifying role as Europeans confront their biggest challenge in decades. The success or failure of the new government will be highly consequential—not least for the political debate that will inform the outcome of Germany's elections in 2013.

October 10, 2012

BACK TO THE BRINK FOR THE EUROZONE?

When European Central Bank President Mario Draghi announced in late July that the ECB would "do whatever it takes" to prevent so-called "re-denomination risk" (the threat that some countries might be forced to give up the euro and reintroduce their own currencies), Spanish and Italian sovereign-bond yields fell immediately. Then, in early September the ECB's Council of Governors endorsed Draghi's vow, further calming markets.

The tide of crisis, it seemed, had begun to turn, particularly after the German Constitutional Court upheld the European Stability Mechanism (ESM), Europe's bailout fund. Despite the ECB's imposition of conditionality on beneficiaries of its "potentially unlimited" bond purchases, financial markets across Europe and the United States staged a major rally.

It seems, however, that the euphoria was short-lived. Yields on Spanish and Italian government bonds have been inching up again, and equity investors' mood is souring. So, what went wrong?

When I welcomed Mario Draghi's strong statement in August, I argued that the ECB's new "outright monetary transactions" (OMT) program needed to be complemented by progress toward a more integrated Eurozone, with a fiscal authority, a banking union, and some form of debt mutualization.[68] The OMT program's success, I argued, presupposed a decisive change in the macroeconomic policy mix throughout the Eurozone.

There has been some progress, albeit slow, toward agreement on the institutional architecture of a more integrated Eurozone. The necessity of a banking union is now more generally accepted, and there is a move to augment the European budget with funds that could be deployed with policy or project conditionality, in addition to ESM resources. (Germany and its northern European allies, however, insist that this be an alternative to some form of debt mutualization, rather than a complement to it.)

The ESM, supported by the ECB, could become a European version of the International Monetary Fund, and the new funds in the European budget could become, with support from the European Investment Bank, Europe's World Bank. All of this will take time, but there is some movement in the right direction.

Where there has been virtually no progress at all is in the recalibration of the macroeconomic policy mix. The prevailing strategy in Europe remains simply to force internal devaluation on the southern countries, with excessive austerity aimed at causing severe wage and price deflation. While some internal devaluation is being achieved, it is producing so much economic and social dislocation—and, increasingly, political upheaval—that there is no supply response, despite the accompanying structural reforms.

Indeed, the deflationary spiral, particularly in Greece and Spain, is causing output to contract so rapidly that further spending cuts and tax increases are not reducing budget deficits and public debt relative to GDP. And Europe's preferred solution—more austerity—is merely causing fiscal targets to recede faster. As a result, markets have again started to measure GDP to include some probability of currency re-denomination, causing debt ratios to look much worse than those based on the certainty of continued euro membership.

While all of this is happening in Europe's south, most of the northern countries are running current-account surpluses. Germany's surplus, at $216 billion, is now larger than China's—and the world's largest in absolute terms. Together with the surpluses of Austria, the Netherlands, and most non-Eurozone northern countries—namely, Switzerland, Sweden, Denmark, and Norway—northern Europe has run a current-account surplus of $511 billion over the last 12 months. That is larger than the Chinese surplus has ever been—and scary because it subtracts net demand from the rest of Europe and the world economy.

Inflicting excessive austerity on the southern European countries while limiting their exports by restricting effective demand in the north is like administering an overdose to a patient while withholding oxygen. The political and economic success of southern Europe's much-needed structural reforms requires the proper dose and timing of budgetary medicine and buoyant demand in the north.

The northern countries argue that permitting wage growth and boosting domestic demand would reduce their competitiveness and trade surplus. But that misses the entire point: surplus countries must contribute no less than deficit countries to global and regional rebalancing, because the world economy cannot export to outer space. This argument was always emphasized when the Chinese surplus was deemed excessive, but it is virtually ignored when it comes to northern Europe.

If conservative politicians and economists in Europe's north continue to insist on the wrong overall macroeconomic policy mix in Europe, they could yet bring about the end of the Eurozone, and, with it, the end of the European project of peace and integration as we have known it for decades. This is not to argue against the need for vigorous structural and competitiveness-enhancing reforms in the south; it is to give those reforms a chance to succeed.

February 4, 2013

DAVID CAMERON'S EUROPEAN SPAGHETTI BOWL

British Prime Minister David Cameron's "Europe" speech, delivered on January 23, was powerful, polished, contained a bold vision, and offered good arguments.[69] In particular, he got three things right. But translating those arguments into institutional reality will be a nearly impossible challenge.

First, Cameron is correct to emphasize the urgent need

for a renewal of popular support for the European Union. The percentage of Europeans who believe that the EU is "a good thing" is dropping steadily.

Democracies require real debate. Yet too many decisions about the future of Europe and the Eurozone are made in highly technocratic settings, with most citizens not really understanding what is going on, let alone feeling that policymakers care. One can debate whether a referendum is the most appropriate vehicle for asking for their consent, but ask one must.

As Cameron put it: "There is a gap between the EU and its citizens which has grown dramatically in recent years and which represents a lack of democratic accountability and consent that is—yes—felt particularly acutely in Britain." Addressing the political challenge head on is much better than trying to evade the debate.

Second, Cameron was right to say that the "European Union that emerges from the Eurozone crisis . . . will be transformed beyond recognition by the measures needed to save the Eurozone." He did not disagree that the Eurozone needs more integration, but correctly noted that the required degree of political integration is beyond the comfort zone of British citizens and of others in the EU.

Finally, Cameron argues that the EU is not an end in itself. Rather, it must deliver better economic performance for its citizens by emphasizing the challenge of competitiveness, particularly with respect to the new emerging countries. His speech stressed the economic weakness of many EU members (though some—such as Germany and the Nordic countries—are actually doing reasonably well in the global marketplace).

As a conservative, Cameron lays the blame for economic weakness on the size of the state and a high degree of market regulation, though some Nordic countries with large government spending and strong financial and environmental regulations are in better shape than the United Kingdom, which has had less of both. But he is right that a debate on economic performance is needed, and that it will be crucial to reform Europe in a way that maximizes its prospects in global competition.

It is normal for conservatives to argue for less government and to place greater trust in free markets, and for Social Democrats and Greens to argue for public policies that deliver less income inequality, more public goods (such as a clean environment and public transport), and more regulation to help markets function with greater stability and distribute benefits more evenly. The competitiveness debate should indeed be part of the debate about Europe's renewal.

But Cameron's vision for Europe's institutional future is difficult to translate into workable specifics. He argues for a Europe "à la carte," at least for those outside the Eurozone. He entertains the possibility that the UK and other EU countries that have opted out of the Eurozone could each negotiate a specific and special "deal" with the EU, picking and choosing among its various dimensions those that suit them best and cost them the least.

Thinking about the consequences that such a Europe would have on EU institutions, one must ask how the European Commission, the European Parliament, and the Council of Ministers would function. Would there be one set of sub-institutions for every country that has made a special deal with the Union—say, a Commission for the Eurozone and Sweden, and another for the Eurozone and the UK?

And would the European Parliament become fragmented in similar fashion? Would the European Council have a diverse set of memberships? How many temporary or permanent opt-outs can there be? How will Europe's citizens, who already have enough trouble with the complexities of European governance, be able to comprehend such a "spaghetti bowl" structure?

And yet Cameron is right to believe that not all EU members will want or be able to be part of a more integrated Eurozone. There will have to be some flexibility if the EU is not to shrink, becoming a smaller Eurozone. British membership is important to many in Europe.

One way to overcome the dilemma might be to articulate an institutional future in which there would be essentially just two types of countries within the EU and the single market: those in the Eurozone and those with national currencies. There would have to be two sets of EU institutions, one for the Eurozone and another for non-Eurozone countries, although they would overlap.

This is already the case in some areas: consider the EU-wide Ecofin and the Eurozone-only Eurogroup of Finance Ministers. Something similar could be created for the European Parliament, and so on. It would be complex, but it could be made manageable; we should discuss how.

A new European treaty would not allow cherry-picking, but would give each member state a chance to join, or commit to, either the politically more integrated Eurozone or the less integrated second group. There would be clear rules and decisionmaking mechanisms for both sets of countries, subject to democratic votes by a two-tier European Parliament.

Many details would have to be worked out. But this may be a vision that gives Europe a chance to remain big and inclusive, while retaining the politically integrated core that the Eurozone needs.

September 16, 2013

THE EUROPEAN CONSEQUENCES OF GERMANY'S ELECTION

Nearly a century ago, in 1919, John Maynard Keynes analyzed the economic consequences of the peace following Germany's defeat in World War I.[70] To be sure, the consequences of Germany's general election on September 22 will not be nearly as momentous. But the outcome will not be as inconsequential as most analysts currently claim.

For starters, even if the current Christian Democratic Union-Free Democrat Party (CDU-FDP) coalition forms the next government, Chancellor Angela Merkel could make longer-term and more courageous decisions without having to worry about the immediate electoral impact. She would be able to pursue a two- or three-year program, instead of her current four-week strategy.

Merkel's postelection agenda might still be very cautious, emphasizing medium-term fiscal consolidation for Germany and the Eurozone as a whole at the expense of boosting employment and growth. But a reelected Merkel would no doubt be willing to proceed, at least by small steps, on the creation of a European banking union, including a resolution mechanism that draws on Eurozone-wide resources.[71]

Moreover, even if Merkel leads the same political coalition, she would more strongly support Eurozone schemes to encourage lending to small and medium-size enterprises, and European Union education programs, such as Erasmus. She would also be willing to work on institutional reforms aimed at closer coordination of EU member states' economic policies.

Finally, even within the CDU-FDP camp, there is growing recognition that Germany's enormous current-account surplus—above 6% of GDP and the world's largest in absolute terms, at about $250 billion—means that Germans receive almost no return on about 25% of their savings.[72] Somewhat faster demand growth in Germany and a lower external surplus would help not only Germany's trade partners, but also German savers.

Of course, the CDU-FDP coalition may not be returned to power. The other postelection scenarios are a grand coalition between the CDU and the Social Democratic Party (SDP); a red-green coalition between the SDP and the Greens (if both do better than predicted and the liberal FDP falls below the 5% electoral threshold), possibly with tacit support from the left-wing Die Linke; or a CDU-Green coalition.

In all three cases, the government would be more oriented toward European and Eurozone integration than a renewed CDU-FDP administration would be. True, the

German Constitutional Court has ruled out open-ended financial commitments over which the German parliament has no control, so Germany can go only so far in support of greater economic integration without greater political integration. But a government that includes the SDP or the Greens would contain at least one party that is ready for more significant steps toward a quasi-federal Eurozone featuring elements of fiscal union (though limited for the sake of constitutional compliance).

Both parties are less complacent than the current government about the Eurozone's stability and Europe's growth prospects. And both believe that there are too many low-paid marginal jobs in Germany to justify glowing reports about the quality of employment; that income growth is too slow and accrues disproportionately to the wealthiest; and that somewhat greater Eurozone solidarity is in Germany's own long-term interest.

The German election will not produce a political earthquake and will not suddenly open the door to a federal Europe on the model of the United States, with large implicit fiscal transfers and highly centralized defense and foreign policies. But, at a minimum, the outcome is likely to speed up implementation of Eurozone decisions that have already been made, leading to somewhat more expansionary economic policies in both Germany and the Eurozone.

A government that includes the SDP or the Greens—both of which have egalitarianism and internationalism in their DNA—would almost certainly go further and embrace substantial reform, renewal, and strengthening of Eurozone institutions as a medium-term target. Such a government would back a Eurozone strategy, led by Germany and France, that focuses on growth and employment, which would infuse some constructive enthusiasm into the 2014 European Parliament election. That would enable Europe, now with the full support of Germany, to recover more rapidly from its economic malaise and to take on the global leadership role that has eluded it for so long.

May 9, 2014

EUROPE'S POLITICAL TRANSCENDENCE

This month, European citizens will head to the polls to select the 751 members of the European Parliament to represent 507 million people. The way the election campaign has unfolded marks a small but significant step in the emergence of the first transnational political space in European—indeed, world—history.

To be sure, the European Parliament elections have been bringing smaller shares of voters to the polls: 43% in 2009, compared to almost 60% in 1978–94. Nonetheless, the participation rate over the last decade is comparable to average turnout in American congressional elections.[73] Given the perceived remoteness of the European Parliament and widespread frustration with the European Union's bureaucracy, the level of participation and the movement toward transnational politics are remarkable.

The transnational nature of the election is stronger this time because the major pan-European political parties have, for the first time, nominated specific candidates for the presidency of the European Commission, and the candidates are campaigning, including in televised debates. The European Council, as mandated by the Lisbon Treaty, will have to take into account the election results in selecting the candidate to put forward for parliamentary endorsement.[74]

The campaign for the Commission's presidency may turn out to be as significant as the final selection. The first debate, held late last month, included Jean-Claude Juncker of the center-right European People's Party (EPP), the Green Party's Ska Keller, Martin Schulz of the center-left Progressive Alliance of Socialists and Democrats, and Guy Verhofstadt of the centrist Alliance of Liberals and Democrats. Alexis Tsipras, representing the Party of the European Left, is expected to participate in the final debate this month.

All of the candidates spoke flawless English—though the debate was translated into 16 languages. Given the United Kingdom's reservations about European integration, it is somewhat ironic that English is playing such a critical role in facilitating the creation of a transnational political space.

The debate attracted significant social-media attention, with tens of thousands of tweets on the subject reflecting the passion that some Europeans—especially the younger generation—feel about Europe's political evolution. More generally, while public interest in the campaign remains far below that seen in national political contests, it has become stronger than in recent pan-European elections, despite the rise of nationalism and Euro-skepticism.

In this context, it would be strange if the European

Council tried to nominate the Commission president without regard for the public's response to the campaign. And yet there is a risk that the selection process becomes no more than an exercise in political horse-trading, with Council members awarding leadership positions, including seats on the Commission, purely on the basis of national political considerations. Such an approach would deal a powerful blow to the citizens who took their European ballot seriously—and to the credibility of the EU as a whole.

Could this really happen? Or has the transnational European space—however young—already grown to the point that it cannot be ignored?

Much will depend on the election results. First and foremost, the participation rate will be critical. If it were to fall below the 43% attained in 2009, the Council could more plausibly argue that the preferences of a decreasingly interested public can be largely ignored. A substantial increase, however—say, toward the 45–47% range—would make it much more difficult to ignore the outcome of the campaign.

The relative performance of the pan-European parties will also matter. If, for example, the Socialists won 215 seats, compared to 185 for the EPP, the substantial difference would make their leader, Martin Schulz, a very strong contender, even though no party came close to an absolute majority of 376 seats.

If the outcome turns out to be closer, with a difference of only five or ten seats between the two top parties, it could be argued that neither of the leading candidates had "won." This would give the Council more space to consider an "outside" candidate (for example, Pascal Lamy, who is closer to the center left, or Christine Lagarde, who is closer to the center right, both of whom are extremely experienced European policymakers whose names have already been raised in the media).

To bolster the legitimacy of such a move, the Council would have to select the candidate more closely associated with the party that gained more votes, however narrow the margin. Moreover, an outside candidate must be likely to generate backing by a sufficiently large coalition in the parliament. Alternatively, with neither of the larger parties able to declare real victory, they could decide as a compromise to indicate preference for one of the other leaders who had campaigned—perhaps Verhofstadt, the liberal centrist.

As Jean Pisani-Ferry has explained, despite the European Parliament's substantial—and increasing—power, it cannot be the central actor in Europe's economic policy debates in the short term.[75] Real decisionmaking power will remain largely national.

But, given the parliament's position at the center of a nascent transnational European space that could, over time, transform Europe's politics and help the continent overcome resurgent and dangerous chauvinism, this first European election with a transnational flavor should not be ignored. When they meet on May 28, European leaders would do well to encourage the strength of European institutions by choosing both competence and legitimacy.

June 12, 2014

DEMOCRACY IN EUROPE

A real struggle over who will preside over the European Commission has begun. Though the center-right European People's Party (EPP) won only a narrow plurality of 221 seats in the 751-seat European Parliament, center-left, Green, and liberal parliament members have all rallied behind the EPP's candidate, Jean-Claude Juncker, as the "legitimate" choice.[76] The opposition, led by British Prime Minister David Cameron with the support of "sovereignists" across Europe, particularly in Scandinavia, but also in Hungary, contends that someone whom the majority of European citizens hardly know cannot claim any kind of political legitimacy.[77]

German Chancellor Angela Merkel is now in a bind. Though she endorsed Juncker before the election, she never really backed the notion that the European Parliament should have a decisive part in selecting the Commission's president. She was certain that no party would win an absolute majority, but she did not foresee that almost all representatives from moderate parties would back whichever candidate won a plurality, making it difficult to appoint anyone else.

The larger issue at stake is whether Europe is prepared to establish the common political space that is needed to manage the monetary union and strengthen the European Union's influence in world affairs.

Most economists agree that in the absence of advanced fiscal-policy coordination and a real banking union, Europe's monetary union cannot succeed. This does not bother the United Kingdom, which has no desire to join the Eurozone. Among Eurozone members, however, the need for greater political integration is broadly accepted, and not just by the economic and political elites.

Moreover, as Russia's recent assertions of power in Ukraine and elsewhere in the former Soviet Union demonstrate, European countries need to deepen their security cooperation and develop a common energy policy. And, though cooperation in areas such as data privacy, financial sector regulation, and climate change may not require the degree of political integration that a common currency does, it would benefit greatly from stronger political cohesion and a more profound sense of shared European identity.

The pan-European parties' nomination of Spitzenkandidaten (lead candidates) for the Commission presidency—and the three direct debates among the nominees—marked the start of building a genuine supranational European political space.[78] Indeed, the endorsement of Juncker by the Social Democrats, the Greens, and the Liberals reflects their belief in the need for such a space. The candidates, particularly Martin Schulz, the leader of the Party of European Socialists, campaigned beyond their national borders.

But Europe still has a long way to go, which is apparent from the fact that only a minority of European citizens followed the campaign. A supranational political space can develop only if European politics gains visibility, influence, and credibility. For this reason, Europe's leaders should reach a compromise on the next Commission president quickly and transparently, thereby dispelling the impression among ordinary citizens that European politics is shaped by a dysfunctional process of behind-the-scenes horse-trading.

As usual, Merkel has a critical role to play. Her endorsement of a candidate whom she knew Cameron would vehemently oppose was a serious mistake, because it strengthened the hand of those in the UK who want to leave the EU.

Merkel must now determine how to forge a compromise that does not discredit the Europe-wide democratic process, which currently has more support in Germany than in any other large European country. To this end, support from Italian Prime Minister Matteo Renzi—whose party won 41% of his country's vote, arguably making him the only real winner at the national level—could help.[79]

The stakes are high—and not just for Europe. The world needs a thriving, cohesive EU to advance democratic principles, facilitate conflict resolution, protect the global commons, promote peace, and build trust across borders. The alternative—already gaining traction—is the resurgence of naked power politics and dangerous xenophobia. Without a shared European political space, everyone will be much worse off.

September 18, 2014

REVAMPING EUROPE'S TATTERED SOCIAL CONTRACT

For most of the beginning of 2014, the Eurozone seemed to be in a state of recovery—weak and unsteady, but nonetheless real. In April, the International Monetary Fund estimated that overall GDP growth would reach 1.2% this year, with slowly declining unemployment, up from its previous forecast of 1% growth.[80] With the threat of unsustainably high interest rates in the countries of the Eurozone periphery having disappeared, the path to moderate recovery was supposedly open, to be followed by some acceleration in growth in 2015.

While it is important not to overreact to quarterly figures, recent data, as well as some of the revised data for the first quarter, are deeply disappointing. The pessimism of two years ago has returned—with good reason.

Italy is in an outright recession, and, far from showing hoped-for signs of vitality, French growth is close to zero. Even Germany's GDP declined in quarterly terms in the first half of the year. Finland, a staunch supporter of firm austerity policies, is in negative territory for the first half of the year.

Nominal interest rates for periphery countries' sovereign debt have remained extremely low, and, even when taking into account expectations of very low inflation (or even deflation), real interest rates are low. The Eurozone now is facing not only a financial crisis, but a stagnation crisis. Tensions with Russia may make recovery even more difficult, and it is unlikely that the Eurozone can attain 1% growth in 2014 without major policy changes.

The European Central Bank has announced that it will offer new monetary-policy support and has decided to use all instruments short of direct quantitative easing (it is still not buying sovereign bonds). But it is far from clear whether the proverbial horse led to water will actually drink.

If growth and employment expectations remain dismal, it will be difficult to rekindle demand, particularly private business investment, no matter how low interest rates are, or how many resources banks have for potential lending. ECB President Mario Draghi's message in his speech last month in Jackson Hole, Wyoming, as well as at his September press conference, was a clear call for more fiscal support to boost effective demand.[81]

The essential economic problem is clear: there is an almost desperate need for more fiscal space in the Eurozone to boost aggregate demand, including more investment in Germany. But there is also a persistent need for deep structural reforms on the supply side, so that fiscal stimulus translates into sustainable long-term growth, not just temporary spurts and further increases in countries' debt ratios.

What the "best" structural reforms actually are remains a matter for debate. But in most countries, they include some combination of tax, labor-market, service-sector, and education reforms, as well as reforms in territorial administration, particularly in France.

These reforms should seek to achieve a thoroughly revamped social contract that reflects the realities of 21st-century demographics and global markets, but that also remains sensitive to Europeans' commitment to distributive fairness and political equality, and ensures that citizens are protected from shocks. It is easy to call for "reforms" without specifying their content or taking into account the social, historical, and political context.

At the same time, it will not be possible to design this new social contract country by country. Europe has become too interwoven in myriad ways—not just in purely financial and economic terms, but also psychologically. It must have come as a surprise to many that it was a German court, not a French one, that banned Uber, the mobile app that is revolutionizing the taxi business.[82]

If the new social contract cannot be forged Europe-wide, it must at least apply to the Eurozone to enable the necessary structural reforms. Otherwise, given that the politics and economics of Eurozone reform are inseparably linked, fiscal expansion could prove to be as ineffective as efforts by monetary policymakers to foster growth.

Italy's finance minister, Pier Carlo Padoan, is rightly pushing for a Eurozone "reform scorecard," which would enable direct comparison among national reforms.[83] But, beyond such a scorecard, the will to overcome the stagnation trap must be more than a sum of national wills. Germany must be reassured by what is happening in France and Italy; conversely, southern Europeans must be able to trust that their efforts will gain additional traction from greater investment throughout the region, particularly in Germany.

A new social contract will not appear out of thin air. Now is the time for the new European Commission to propose—and the new European Council and European Parliament to endorse—a political pact to legitimize and sustain the reforms needed to solve Europe's economic problems.

November 14, 2014

EUROPE'S FRANCO-GERMAN DREAM TEAM

When the International Monetary Fund lowered its global growth forecast for 2014 and 2015 from 3.7% and 3.9%, respectively, to 3.3% and 3.8%, it cited the Eurozone's increasingly gloomy prospects, including significantly slower growth in Germany, as a leading cause.[84] After all, the Eurozone still accounts for about 13% of world output at market prices—about the same as China.

Europe's economic struggles are reflected in its political situation, with many European electorates now mired in a sense of hopelessness and sliding toward ideological extremes. But a forthcoming report by two highly respected economists—Jean Pisani-Ferry, the French government's commissioner-general for policy planning, and Henrik Enderlein, a key leader of a reformist group of German economists—will propose a way forward.

The task facing Pisani-Ferry and Enderlein is to create a new reform strategy for Europe's two largest economies, focusing on structural reforms in France and increased investment in Germany. The hope is that the report, which will be made public on December 1, will provide a breakthrough that can revive, at long last, the Eurozone's growth engine.

The paper was commissioned a few days after the IMF's Annual Meetings last month, at a gathering of the French finance and economy ministers, Michel Sapin and Emmanuel Macron, and their German counterparts, Wolfgang Schäuble and Sigmar Gabriel. Though the meeting produced no concrete policy action—as the French daily *Le Monde* put it, "Nothing was asked for, and nothing was obtained"—it could signal the beginning of more effective Franco-German cooperation, guided by the Pisani-Ferry/Enderlein report.

Such cooperation could not come at a better time. A couple of weeks after the project was initiated, France and Italy submitted revised annual budgets to the European Commission, in which they demanded more fiscal room for maneuver. The Commission now has until the end of this month to determine whether France has pursued reform diligently enough to avoid penalties for breaking its pledge to cut its budget deficit to less than 3% of GDP by next year.

An effective reform strategy would have to balance the need for budget restraint and macroeconomic stability with growth-enhancing policies. When it comes to the latter, European Central Bank President Mario Draghi's proposals in August—expanded monetary easing, structural reforms (particularly in France and Italy), and some fiscal expansion by countries like Germany—provide a useful framework to be supplemented with concrete measures.[85]

The ECB governing council has already agreed, in principle, to use the first of these policy tools. But monetary expansion alone will be inadequate to lift the Eurozone out of stagnation.

Moreover, many of the structural reforms that are currently being considered or implemented, despite boosting growth in the long term, can have short-term contractionary effects. This is particularly true of greater labor-market flexibility, a key asset for long-term growth that can lead to a short-term increase in unemployment. That is why a more expansionary fiscal stance is also vital, with Germany leading the way in deploying increased public investment to "crowd in" private investment and boost competitiveness. The IMF's recent *World Economic Outlook* describes the success of this approach in recessionary environments.[86]

Given that Germany and even France can borrow at record-low interest rates, any reasonably well-designed investment program will strengthen the public sector's balance sheet. And, with the Eurozone running a current-account surplus of nearly $350 billion—which the euro's recent decline will bolster further—there is no risk of a Eurozone-wide balance-of-payments crisis.

The key is confidence. Germany must trust that its agreement to loosen the Eurozone's fiscal belt will not lead to a slowdown of structural reforms, and countries like France need to know that excessive austerity will not exacerbate the impact of politically difficult structural reforms in the short run.

In this sense, top-level political support, voiced in a way that elicits the approval of Europe's citizens, will be crucial. Gabriel and Macron must lead the charge, backed by Sapin and Schäuble. Crucially, German Chancellor Angela Merkel and French Prime Minister Manuel Valls—not to mention the new Commission—must also step in to offer genuine support for the project.

Waning confidence is a Eurozone-wide problem, but the Franco-German relationship lies at its core. And, as experience has shown, Germany and France can have a major impact when they work together. The power of that relationship is what the Pisani-Ferry/Enderlein initiative represents—and what could, with sufficient political support, revitalize Europe.

January 21, 2015

STILL NO EXIT FOR GREECE

Opinion polls in the run-up to Greece's early general election on January 25 indicate that the left-wing Syriza party is likely to win the largest share of votes. As a result, Syriza stands to earn a crucial premium under Greek electoral law, according to which the party that gains the most votes is allocated an extra 50 of the parliament's 300 seats. In other words, Syriza could come to power with enormous implications for Greece and Europe.

Syriza is more a coalition than a unified party, meaning that its leader, Alexis Tsipras, must reconcile moderate socialists, including some of his economic advisers, with radical left-wing members. The implementation and impact of Syriza's agenda, especially its decisive economic program, will depend on the new government's ability to maintain support at home and compromise with Greece's creditors abroad.

Syriza's economic program rejects the austerity policies supported—or, some might say, imposed—by the so-called troika (the International Monetary Fund, the European Central Bank, and the European Commission). These policies require Greece to maintain a very high primary budget surplus—more than 4% of GDP—for many years to come.

Syriza also plans to demand a substantial reduction in Greece's foreign debt, the nominal value of which remains very high—close to 170% of GDP. In fact, the real present value of the debt is much lower, given that most of it is now held by governments or other public entities and carries long maturities and low interest rates. Nonetheless, repayment "spikes" this year constitute a real short-term challenge.

The problem for Greece is that its creditors may adopt a very tough stance. This largely reflects the belief that, if a breakdown of negotiations triggers another Greek crisis, the systemic risks to the Eurozone and the wider European Union would be far smaller than they were just a few years ago. The "acute" phase of the euro crisis is over; even if growth remains elusive, financial contagion is no longer viewed as a risk. After all, private creditors hold only a minimal share of Greek debt nowadays. In 2010–12, by contrast, systemically important European banks were exposed, raising the risk of a domino effect that threatened the entire Eurozone.

Moreover, a debt reduction in the form of further

interest-rate reductions and maturity extensions on foreign government–held debt would not hurt financial markets. But debt held by the European Central Bank and the IMF could pose a problem. If Greece's new government does not tread lightly in these discussions, withdrawal of these institutions' liquidity support for Greek banks could follow.

Despite the lack of significant financial contagion risk, a renewed Greek crisis, stemming from a lasting and serious breakdown of negotiations between the new government and EU institutions, would constitute a major problem for European cooperation. The absence of financial contagion would not rule out serious political repercussions.

Europe's political landscape is changing. Populist parties, both on the far right and the far left, are gaining electoral traction. Some, such as France's National Front, oppose their country's Eurozone membership; others, such as Podemos in Spain, do not. Nonetheless, the challenge that these new parties pose to Europe could prove to be extremely disruptive.

A Greek exit from the Eurozone, together with financial and political turmoil inside Greece, would be perceived as a major defeat for European integration—especially after the laborious efforts made to hold together the monetary union and, with it, the European dream. Such an outcome would be even more disheartening in light of the tragic terrorist attacks in Paris in January, and after unity marches in France and across the continent rekindled a long-fading sense of European solidarity.

A new image of solidarity is precisely what the Greek election should produce. There is little doubt that the suffering that Greeks have had to endure for the last five years is mainly attributable to the fiscal profligacy and poor public management of a procession of Greek governments. But as most analysts, including at the IMF, now agree, the troika's approach was also deeply flawed, as it emphasized wage and income cuts, while neglecting the reform of product markets and the dismantling of harmful public and private oligopolies.[87]

For the sake of Greece and Europe, the new government must work with the European institutions to revise their strategy, while taking responsibility for implementing growth-promoting structural reforms. Greece's creditors and partners, for their part, must provide the fiscal space needed for the reforms to work. Walking away from Greece because it no longer poses a threat of financial contagion is not a politically viable option. Both sides will have to show more foresight.

The last five years have provided two clear lessons for Europe: procrastination only makes reform more difficult, and the end of financial turmoil does not necessarily mean the end of socioeconomic crisis. It is time to use these lessons to develop a cooperative strategy that will finally enable Greece to make real progress toward a more stable future. A Greek exit from the euro is not a more viable solution today than it was three years ago.

February 18, 2015

FISCAL AUSTERITY VERSUS EUROPEAN SOCIETY

Over the last five years, the Eurozone has, without explicit popular consent, maintained a strict policy focus on fiscal austerity and structural reforms—despite serious social repercussions, not only in the Mediterranean periphery and Ireland, but even in a "core" European Union country like France. Unless Eurozone leaders rethink their approach, the radical Syriza party's success in Greece's recent general election could turn out to be just one more step toward a future of social fragmentation and political instability in Europe. Or it could mark the beginning of a realistic and beneficial reorientation of Europe's economic strategy.

Of course, fiscal sustainability is vital to prevent a disruptive debt refinancing and inspire confidence among investors and consumers. But there is no denying that it is much easier to support fiscal austerity when one is wealthy enough not to rely on public services or be at serious risk of becoming mired in long-term unemployment. (The wealthy also remain largely in control of the media, the public discourse, and cross-border capital flows.)

For the millions of workers—and especially young people—with no job prospects, fiscal sustainability simply cannot be the only priority. When unemployment benefits are slashed, they are the ones who suffer. And when budget cuts extend to education, it is their children who are unable to gain the skills they need to reach their future potential.

Austerity-induced suffering is particularly extreme

in Greece. Severe pension cuts are preventing the elderly from living out their lives with dignity. A large burden has been placed on those who actually pay their taxes, while many—often the wealthiest, who long ago stashed their money abroad—continue to evade their obligations. Health care has lapsed, with many cancer patients losing access to life-saving treatment. Suicides are on the rise.

Yet Greece's creditors have continued to ignore these developments. This is clearly not sustainable—a point that Reza Moghadam, former director of the International Monetary Fund's Europe Department, recognized when he recently called for writing off half of Greece's debt, provided an agreement can be reached on credible growth-enhancing structural reforms.[88]

Social sustainability is essential for long-term economic success. A country cannot prosper if its educational system lacks the resources and capacity to prepare its children to thrive in the digital economy. Likewise, a reform program cannot be implemented if inequality, poverty, and social frustration strengthen extremist political parties, such as Greece's overtly fascist Golden Dawn party or France's far-right, anti-Europe National Front, which now boasts 25% electoral support.

When times are tough, immigrants and minorities become easy targets. As Joseph Stiglitz recently pointed out, it is unlikely that Hitler would have come to power in Germany if the unemployment rate were not 30% at the time.[89] It does not help when some of those trapped in the poor ghettos surrounding major cities—however small a minority—become tempted by violence and fall prey to terrorist recruiters.

Regardless of what today's corporate profit reports and stock indexes may show, a country cannot achieve inclusive, sustainable success—in economic or human terms—if these fundamental social issues are not adequately addressed. Of course, fiscal caution cannot be abandoned; after all, if governments or the private sector were to spend borrowed or newly minted money freely, the result would simply be more crises, which would hurt the poor most. But social sustainability must be an integral part of a country's economic program, not an afterthought.

The persistent tendency to pay lip service to social sustainability, while implementing economic programs focused on unrelenting austerity, is a leading cause of political instability in Europe. Though reform programs aimed at building viable macroeconomic frameworks remain essential, they must include strong provisions for countercyclical policies to offset the "paradox of thrift" (the tendency to save more during a recession, undermining economic growth). When aggregate demand falls short of aggregate supply, governments must increase public spending.

Moreover, governments that are now focused narrowly on microeconomic issues need to devote the same level of attention and commitment to designing and implementing social policies that focus explicitly on ensuring the livelihoods, health, education, and housing of the most vulnerable segments of the population. And, using new technology to analyze large amounts of data, they should boost the efficiency of social programs, while encouraging the active participation of concerned citizens.

The European Commission and the IMF have admitted their errors—not only the inaccurate macroeconomic forecasts on which the Greek program was based, but also the decision not to account for social sustainability—and have acknowledged that the program has not produced the expected results. Yet, for some reason, Greece's creditors refuse to negotiate with the new government (which enjoys strong domestic support) to develop a new program that incorporates debt relief, a lower fiscal surplus, and structural reforms that support growth and promote social cohesion. This must not continue.

The last five years have underscored the challenge of achieving financial stability. But political and social stability have proved to be even more elusive. Policymakers must direct just as much effort and resources toward realizing social sustainability as they do toward getting the Basel III financial reforms right. Europe's future prosperity—and its global role—depends on it.[90]

September 21, 2015

E PLURIBUS EUROPE?

The European Union's economic crises of the last half-decade have fueled the emergence of a deep divide between the northern creditor countries and the southern debtors. Now Europe's migrant crisis is creating an east-west divide between those countries that welcome the ongoing influx of refugees, and those that want to do little, or nothing, to help. Add to that the growing political divisions within member countries, and one must ask: Is the EU coming unglued?

The creditor/debtor split was thrown into sharp relief this summer, during the negotiations over Greece's third bailout agreement. Germany, the leading proponent of austerity and the most influential creditor, was accused of insufficient flexibility and solidarity; Greece, for its part, was lambasted for failing to implement the reforms that it promised the first two times it was bailed out. (It was France, neither entirely "north" nor entirely "south," that ended up playing a vital role in facilitating the deal.)

Germany is now trying to lead the way in the migrant crisis as well, but this time by its generosity. Chancellor Angela Merkel has pledged to take in more than 800,000 refugees just this year. Welcoming crowds have lined streets and filled train stations in German cities, offering drinks, food, and clothing to the exhausted refugees, many of whom have walked hundreds of miles and risked their lives to get to safety.

Whereas Merkel declared forcefully that Islam was also a religion of Germany, some in eastern Europe have declared that they will welcome only a small number of refugees—and only if they are Christian. Such bigotry plays directly into the hands of Islamist extremists worldwide.

The refugee crisis is all the more challenging in view of EU member countries' internal political fragmentation.[91] While those on the left support cautious acceptance of refugees, the further one moves to the right, the more negative the attitude becomes. Even the Christian Social Union, the Bavarian sister party to Merkel's Christian Democratic Union, has proved a reluctant partner in this area.

Yet another divide lies between the United Kingdom and the rest of the EU. Given the UK's role, alongside France, as the key force in European defense and a significant authority in world affairs, particularly with regard to climate- and development-related issues, the prospect of a genuine split should be a source of serious concern for the EU.

These divisions have created deep doubts about the dream of ever-closer union in Europe, underpinned by a shared system of governance that allows for more effective decisionmaking. Likewise, they are not conducive to implementation of the reforms that are needed to spur economic growth.

Yet it is still too early to write off progress toward increased European integration. In fact, when it comes to EU cohesion, more cleavages are probably better than a single divide.

When economic considerations alone were dominating the debate, austerity-obsessed northern Europe, oblivious to any Keynesian considerations, and struggling southern Europe, desperately in need of fiscal room to make demand-boosting, job-creating structural reforms politically feasible, were at loggerheads. The situation became so heated that some respected observers even proposed creating a "northern euro" for the region around Germany, and a "southern euro" in the Mediterranean (where France would fit was unclear).

In such a Eurozone, the European Central Bank would have to split, and the northern euro would appreciate.

Exchange-rate uncertainty would reappear, not only between the two euros, but also, before long, within the "northern" and "southern" zones, owing to the collapse of confidence in the very idea of a currency union. Within the northern bloc, Germany would play an even more outsize role than it does now, a situation that would likely generate new tensions.

Similarly, a clear division between a refugee friendly west and a closed east would effectively end the Schengen Agreement, because the political disagreement would harden into a physical barrier blocking the free movement of people within the EU.[92] Such a split would be as damaging to Europe's cohesion as a divided Eurozone.

But what if countries that are on opposite sides of one cleavage are on the same side of another? Germany, Italy, Spain, and Sweden may agree on the immigration issue, while Greece, France, Italy, and Portugal agree on Eurozone macroeconomic policies. France, Poland, and the UK may be willing to spend more on defense, while Germany remains more pacifist. And Germany, the Scandinavian countries, and the UK may be at the forefront of the fight against climate change.

Moreover, the Europe-wide political "families" of Christian Democrats, Social Democrats, and so on could be allies on some policies and opponents on others, transcending national or regional borders, and moving toward pan-European politics, with the European Parliament increasing its democratic debate and oversight functions.

A Europe where countries do not fit neatly into one category or another, and where flexible coalitions emerge on various issues, probably has a greater chance of progressing than one divided simply between north and south or east and west. Of course, there remains the challenge of strengthening institutions so that they can manage this diversity and reconcile it with political effectiveness. Here, greater scope for weighted and double-majority voting is crucial. But, for truly democratic societies, the challenge of reconciling divergent interests never goes away.

November 10, 2015

TWO EUROPES IN ONE

Informal discussions on the United Kingdom's relationship with the European Union are now under way. With a referendum on the UK's continued EU membership set to take place before the end of 2016, the talks are the first step toward negotiating changes that, EU leaders hope, will convince British voters to choose Europe.

And changes will certainly be needed. Indeed, as Prime Minister David Cameron is well aware, given the current dynamic of the UK's relationship with the EU, British voters would undoubtedly choose to leave the EU.

But Cameron also knows that he must handle the negotiations with care. If he asks for more than the EU can accommodate, he will look as if he caved in. If he asks for too little, Britain's Euroskeptics will have more fuel for their campaign against continued membership.

Likewise, if EU leaders give Cameron too much— allowing the UK to reap the benefits of membership, without shouldering the same responsibilities as its partners—their populations could turn on them. But if they give too little, they could lose the UK as a partner.

Beyond such tactical matters, the UK and its European partners must address long-term issues relating to the changing shape of the Eurozone. The euro crisis has given rise to a consensus that, in order to function effectively, the Eurozone must pursue further integration. Specific proposals include a designated Eurozone budget, increased fiscal-policy coordination among members, and a Eurozone finance minister.

For the UK, which opted out of the euro, this is a cause for concern, as it could leave the country on the sidelines of major decisionmaking processes—especially if the necessary shift toward weighted majority voting removes the need for unanimity in more areas. Cameron already has pressed for an "emergency brake" mechanism to slow down decisions on issues that are important to the non-euro countries.

Clearly, the need for much greater Eurozone integration must be balanced against some countries' strong desire to preserve more national sovereignty than is feasible in the monetary union. The best way to do this would be to divide Europe into two groups. Inclusion in one or the other would be based not on the potential "speed" of integration, but on a country's permanent (or at least long-term) decision on adopting the euro.

Of course, to some extent, this is already the EU's fundamental structure. But establishing this categorical division—beginning with, as the UK has requested, an explicit recognition that the EU is a multicurrency union—would allow for the creation of a decisionmaking framework that better protects both groups' interests.

The non-euro group—including Britain, Denmark, Sweden, Poland, and some other eastern European countries—would continue to elect representatives to the European Parliament and participate fully in EU institutions. Meanwhile, the euro group would pursue far greater fiscal integration, in addition to their current cooperation. To ensure democratic legitimacy and satisfy national constitutional courts (not least Germany's), a second European parliament would have to be established to serve as the Eurozone's legislative branch.

This new Eurozone parliament could be formed either by a subset of members of the larger European Parliament, or by some combination of representatives from the European Parliament and national parliaments. The proposed finance minister, responsible for overseeing fiscal policy in the monetary union, would be responsible to the Eurozone parliament.

Full realization of this vision would require either a change to the existing European treaties or, more feasible, agreement by Eurozone members on a new treaty, like the "fiscal compact" that entered into force in 2013. In the meantime, Article 136 of the existing Treaty on the Functioning of the EU would allow for some preliminary steps, such as the designation of votes at the European Council that are reserved for Eurozone countries only.[93]

Establishing "two Europes in one," rather than a "two-speed Europe," would allow Europe to organize itself in a lasting way. The more federal Eurozone would be embedded in a larger union that cooperates on defense, foreign policy, climate-change measures, and migration policy. Free movement of European citizens within the EU would be upheld.

This system would allow those who do not wish to share monetary sovereignty, or engage in the kind of fiscal cooperation that must eventually come with it, to make that choice. At the same time, it would avoid the complications of having multiple Europes—an option that may be attractive to veteran Eurocrats from a purely functional perspective, but soon becomes hopelessly complicated. A political system's clarity and comprehensibility, together with its voluntary nature, are essential to democratic legitimacy.

Of course, this process will be long, and many details remain to be worked out. But important progress can be made by the time the UK's referendum is held—if, that is, EU leaders begin pursuing this goal in earnest now. The talks being held are an opportunity that neither side can afford to miss.

NOTES

1. Robert J. Gordon, *The Rise and Fall of American Growth: The U.S. Standard of Living since the Civil War* (Princeton University Press, 2016).

2. Facundo Alvaredo, Tony Atkinson, Thomas Piketty, Emmanuel Saez, and Gabriel Zucman, "The World Wealth and Income Database," November 30, 2015 (www.wid.world).

3. Lawrence H. Summers, "U.S. Economic Prospects: Secular Stagnation, Hysteresis, and the Zero Lower Bound," *Business Economics* 49 (2014), pp. 65–73.

4. Robert J. Gordon, *The Rise and Fall of American Growth: The U.S. Standard of Living since the Civil War* (Princeton University Press, 2016).

5. International Monetary Fund, "Growth Resuming, Dangers Remain," *World Economic Outlook*, 2012.

6. U.S. Bureau of Labor Statistics, "Labor Force Statistics from Population Survey," U.S. Department of Commerce; EurostatDatabase, "Unemployment Rate by Sex and Age—Monthly Average," European Commission, 2012.

7. Consolidated Version of the Treaty on the Functioning of the European Union, 2012, O.J./C 326/01, Chapter 2: Monetary Policy, Article 127 (ex Article 105 TEC) (http://eur-lex.europa.eu/legal-content/EN/TXT/?uri=CELEX:12012E/TXT).

8. Jeffrey Frankel, "Time for Nominal Growth Targets," Project Syndicate, December 16, 2012 (www.project-syndicate. org/commentary/monetary-policy-should-target-nominal-gdp-growth-by-jeffrey-frankel).

9. See "Mario Draghi's Guns of August" in this collection.

10. European Commission, Eurostat Database, "Long Term Government Bond Yields," Eurostat Database, 2012.

11. International Monetary Fund, "Gradual Upturn in Global Growth During 2013," *World Economic Outlook: Update*, January 23, 2013 (www.imf.org/external/pubs/ft/weo/2013/update/01/index.htm).

12. U.S. Bureau of Labor Statistics, "Labor Force Statistics from Population Survey," U.S. Department of Labor, 2012.

13. Carmen DeNavas-Walt, Bernadette D. Proctor, and Jessica C. Smith, "Income, Poverty, and Health Insurance Coverage in the United States: 2011," Current Population Reports, pp. 60–243, U.S. Department of Commerce, September 2012 (www.census.gov/prod/2012pubs/p60-243.pdf).

14. Arvind Subramanian, *Eclipse: Living in the Shadow of China's Economic Dominance* (Washington: Peterson Institute of International Economics, 2011); Uri Dadush and William Shaw, *Juggernaut: How Emerging Markets Are Reshaping Globalization* (Washington: Carnegie Endowment for International Peace, 2011).

15. Dani Rodrik, "The Future of Economic Convergence," Working Paper No. 17400 (Cambridge, Mass.: National Bureau of Economic Research, September 2011) (www.nber.org/papers/w17400.pdf).

16. See "A World of Convergence" in this collection.

17. Cesar A. Hidalgo and Ricardo Hausmann, "The Building Blocks of Economic Complexity," *Proceedings of the National Academy of Sciences of the United States of America*, edited by Partha Sarathi Dasgupta, University of Cambridge, May 1, 2009 (http://

chidalgo.com/Papers/HidalgoHausmann_PNAS_2009_PaperAndSM.pdf).

18. Ricardo Hausmann, "The End of the Emerging-Market Party," Project Syndicate, August 30, 2013 (www.project-syndicate.org/commentary/the-reversal-of-nominal-gdp-growth-in-emerging-countries-by-ricardo-hausmann).

19. Ernesto Talvi, "Latin America's Irrational Exuberance," Project Syndicate, November 12, 2013 (www.project-syndicate.org/commentary/ernesto-talvi-on-the-underlying-weakness-of-latin-america-s-economies).

20. Board of Governors of the Federal Reserve System, "Federal Reserve 2014 Monetary Policy Releases," January 29, 2014 (www.federalreserve.gov/newsevents/press/monetary/20140129a.htm).

21. Federal Reserve Bank of St. Louis, "Balance on Current Account," FRED Economic Database, 2013.

22. Dani Rodrik, "No More Growth Miracles," Project Syndicate, August 8, 2012 (www.project-syndicate.org/commentary/no-more-growth-miracles-by-dani-rodrik).

23. Erik Brynjolfsson and Andrew McAfee, *The Second Machine Age: Work, Progress, and Prosperity in a Time of Brilliant Technologies* (New York: W. W. Norton & Company, 2014).

24. Thomas Piketty, *Capital in the Twenty-First Century* (Harvard University Press, 2014).

25. Christopher B. Field and others, "Climate Change 2014: Impacts, Adaptation, and Vulnerability: Summary for Policymakers," Intergovernmental Panel on Climate Change, 2014 (http://ipcc-wg2.gov/AR5/images/uploads/WG2AR5_SPM_FINAL.pdf).

26. Organization of the Petroleum Exporting Countries, "OPEC Basket Price," OPEC Database, 2013.

27. Fifth Assessment Report (AR5), approved by IPPC-31, Intergovernmental Panel on Climate Change, 2013 (www.ipcc.ch/pdf/ar5/ar5-outline-compilation.pdf).

28. UNFCCC Lima Climate Change Conference, Lima, Peru, December 1–14, 2014.

29. Simon Johnson, "How to Fight Currency Manipulation," Project Syndicate, March 24, 2015 (www.project-syndicate.org/commentary/currency-manipulation-fight-by-simon-johnson-2015-03); "Overview of the Trans-Pacific Partnership: Increasing American Exports, Supporting American Jobs," Office of the United States Trade Representative, 2013 (https://ustr.gov/tpp/overview-of-the-TPP); C. Fred Bergsten, "The Truth about Currency Manipulation," *Foreign Affairs*, January 18, 2015 (www.foreignaffairs.com/articles/united-states/2015-01-18/truth-about-currency-manipulation).

30. International Monetary Fund, "IMF Executive Board Adopts New Decision on Bilateral Surveillance over Members' Policies," Public Information Notice (PIN) No. 07/69, June 21, 2007 (www.imf.org/external/np/sec/pn/2007/pn0769.htm).

31. International Monetary Fund, "2014 Triennial Surveillance Review," December 16, 2014 (www.imf.org/external/np/spr/triennial/2014/).

32. B. Douglas Bernheim, "Ricardian Equivalence: An Evaluation of Theory and Evidence," Working Paper No. 2330, Reprint No. r1008 (Cambridge, Mass.: National Bureau of Economic Research, July 1987) (www.nber.org/papers/w2330).

33. Stefan Kawalec, "Europe's Currency Manipulation," Project Syndicate, April 1, 2015 (www.project-syndicate.org/commentary/euro-currency-manipulation-by-stefan-kawalec-2015-04).

34. Andrew McAfee, interview by Laureline Savoye for Rencontres Économiques forum, Le Cercle des Économistes, Aix-en-Provence, July 4, 2015 (http://lesrencontreseconomiques.fr/2015/?lang=en).

35. John Maynard Keynes, "Economic Possibilities for Our Grandchildren," in *Essays in Persuasion* (New York: W. W. Norton & Co., 1963), pp. 358–73.

36. Jean Pisani-Ferry, "The End of Work as We Know It," Project Syndicate, July 1, 2015 (www.project-syndicate.org/commentary/uber-automation-labor-markets-by-jean-pisani-ferry-2015-07).

37. See "The Future of Economic Progress" in this collection.

38. Thomas Piketty, *Capital in the Twenty-First Century* (Harvard University Press, 2014).

39. Lawrence H. Summers, "Economic Possibilities for Our Children," Fifth Annual Martin Feldstein Lecture, NBER Reporter 2013 No. 4, National Bureau of Economic Research, Cambridge, Mass., July 24, 2013 (www.nber.org/reporter/2013number4/2013no4.pdf).

40. Neil Irwin, *The Alchemists: Three Central Bankers and a World on Fire* (Penguin Books: 2013).

41. Margaret MacMillan, "The Rhyme of History: Lessons of the Great War," Brookings Institution, December 14, 2013 (www.brookings.edu/research/essays/2013/rhyme-of-history).

42. Basel Committee on Banking Supervision, "Basel III: A Global Regulatory Framework for More Resilient Banks and Banking Systems," Bank for International Settlements, December 2010 (rev. June 2011). (www.bis.org/publ/bcbs189.pdf).

43. Facundo Alvaredo, Tony Atkinson, Thomas Piketty, Emmanuel Saez, and Gabriel Zucman, "The World Wealth and Income Database," 2014 (www.wid.world).

44. Lawrence H. Summers, "Book Reviews: The Inequality Puzzle," *Democracy* 33 (Summer 2014) (http://democracyjournal.org/magazine/33/the-inequality-puzzle/).

45. Lawrence H. Summers, "Economic Possibilities for Our Children," Fifth Annual Martin Feldstein Lecture, NBER Reporter 2013 No. 4 (Cambridge, Mass.: National Bureau of Economic Research, July 24, 2013) (www.nber.org/reporter/2013number4/2013no4.pdf).

46. Carl Benedikt Frey and Michael A. Osborne, "The

Future of Employment: How Susceptible Are Jobs to Computerisation?," University of Oxford, September 17, 2013 (www.oxfordmartin.ox.ac.uk/downloads/academic/The_Future_of_Employment.pdf).

47. Jeremy Greenwood, Nezih Guner, Georgi Kocharkov, and Cezar Santos, "Marry Your Like: Assortative Mating and Income Inequality," Working Paper No. 19829 (Cambridge, Mass.: National Bureau of Economic Research, January 2014) (www.nber.org/papers/w19829.pdf?new_window=1).

48. Michael Spence, "The Global Security Deficit," Project Syndicate, July 25, 2014 (www.project-syndicate.org/commentary/michael-spence-warns-that-political-instability-and-conflict-are-now-the-main-threat-to-the-global-economy).

49. International Monetary Fund, "An Uneven Global Recovery Continues," *World Economic Outlook: Update*, July 2014 (www.imf.org/external/pubs/ft/weo/2014/update/02/).

50. Christopher M. Clark, *The Sleepwalkers: How Europe Went to War in 1914* (New York: HarperCollins, 2013).

51. International Monetary Fund, "IMF Board Approves Far-Reaching Governance Reforms," *IMF Survey Magazine*, November 5, 2010 (www.imf.org/external/pubs/ft/survey/so/2010/NEW110510B.htm).

52. "Sixth Summit: Fortaleza Declaration and Action Plan," BRICS, 2014 (http://brics.itamaraty.gov.br/category-english/21-documents/223-sixth-summit-declaration-and-action-plan).

53. Gideon Rachman, "Viktor Orban's Illiberal World," *Financial Times*, July 30, 2014 (http://blogs.ft.com/the-world/2014/07/viktor-orbans-illiberal-world/?Authorised=false).

54. Dani Rodrik, "From Welfare State to Innovation State," Project Syndicate, January 14, 2014 (www.project-syndicate.org/commentary/labor-saving-technology-by-dani-rodrik-2015-01).

55. Jeffrey Sachs, "The Drug That Is Bankrupting America,"

Huffington Post, February 16, 2015 (www.huffingtonpost.com/jeffrey-sachs/the-drug-that-is-bankrupt_b_6692340.html).

56. Organization for Economic Cooperation and Development, "Gross Domestic Expenditure on R-D by Sector of Performance and Source of Funds," OECD Statistics, 2014.

57. G20 Leaders' Communiqué, Brisbane Summit, November 15–16, 2014 (www.g20australia.org/sites/default/files/g20_resources/library/brisbane_g20_leaders_summit_communique.pdf).

58. Mohamed A. El-Erian, "Western Politics' Locust Years," Project Syndicate, May 11, 2015 (www.project-syndicate.org/commentary/us-europe-political-polarization-by-mohamed-a--el-erian-2015-05).

59. "Manhood: Men Adrift, " *The Economist*, May 21, 2015 (www.economist.com/news/essays/21649050-badly-educated-men-rich-countries-have-not-adapted-well-trade-technology-or-feminism).

60. Jonathan Hall and Alan Krueger, "An Analysis of the Labor Market for Uber's Driver-Partners in the United States," Industrial Relations Section Working Paper No. 587, Princeton University, January 22, 2015 (http://dataspace.princeton.edu/jspui/bitstream/88435/dsp010z708z67d/5/587.pdf).

61. See "The Paradox of Identity Politics" in this collection.

62. Jan-Emmanuel De Nevea and Andrew J. Oswald, "Estimating the Influence of Life Satisfaction and Positive Affect on Later Income Using Sibling Fixed Effects," *Proceedings of the National Academy of Sciences of the United States of America*, edited by Jose A. Scheinkman, Princeton University, July 10, 2012 (www.pnas.org/content/109/49/19953.full.pdf).

63. Stefan Zweig, *The World of Yesterday* (London: Cassell, 1953).

64. Francis Fukuyama, "The End of History?," *The National Interest*, Summer 1989.

65. International Monetary Fund, "Latest IMF Projections," *World Economic Outlook*, October 2015 (www.imf.org/external/pubs/ft/weo/2015/02/images/Overview.jpg).

66. See "Austere Growth?" in this collection.

67. International Monetary Fund, "Euro Area Policies," IMF Country Report No.12/181, July 3, 2012 (www.imf.org/external/pubs/ft/scr/2012/cr12181.pdf).

68. See "Mario Draghi's Guns of August" in this collection.

69. David Cameron, EU Referendum speech, given at Bloomberg's European headquarters, London, January 23, 2013 (www.gov.uk/government/speeches/eu-speech-at-bloomberg).

70. John Maynard Keynes, *The Economic Consequences of the Peace* (New York: Harcourt, Brace and Howe, 1920).

71. European Commission, "Vienna 2 Initiative: Working Group on the European Banking Union and Emerging Europe," April 30, 2013 (http://ec.europa.eu/economy_finance/financial_operations/coordination/eif/documents/vi2_bu_wg_april_2013_en.pdf).

72. Eurostat Database, "Balance of the Current Account," European Commission, 2013; Daniel Gros, "The World Economy According to an Excess Savings Country," Think Tank 20: The G-20 and Central Banks in the New World of Unconventional Monetary Policy, Brookings Institution, August 2013, pp. 38-40 (www.brookings.edu/~/media/Research/Files/Reports/2013/08/g20%20central%20banks%20monetary%20policy/TT20%20germany_gros.pdf).

73. European Parliament, "Results of the 2014 European Elections," 2014 (www.europarl.europa.eu/elections2014-results/en/election-results-2014.html); U.S. Census Bureau, Voting and Registration: Historical Time Series Tables (A-1/10), 2014 (www.census.gov/hhes/www/socdemo/voting/publications/historical/index.html).

74. Treaty of Lisbon: Amending the Treaty on European

Union and the Treaty Establishing the European Community, [2007] O.J./C 306/01 (http://ec.europa.eu/archives/lisbon_treaty/full_text/index_en.htm).

75. Jean Pisani-Ferry, "Europe's Trapped Politics," Project Syndicate, April 29, 2014 (www.project-syndicate.org/commentary/jean-pisani-ferry-doubts-that-the-european-parliament-election-can-address-growing-divergences-among-eu-members).

76. European Parliament, "Results of the 2014 European Elections," 2014 (www.europarl.europa.eu/elections2014-results/en/election-results-2014.html).

77. Gideon Rachman, "Block Juncker to Save Real Democracy in Europe," *Financial Times*, June 2, 2014 (www.ft.com/intl/cms/s/0/c0fae448-ea38-11e3-8dde-00144feabdc0.html#axzz40SlT4rXk).

78. Jean-Claude Juncker, Martin Schulz, Guy Verhofstadt, and Ska Keller, "The First European Presidential Debate," Maastricht, April 28, 2014 (debate between EU presidential candidates). (www.euronews.com/2014/04/14/what-will-you-ask-the-potential-future-president-of-the-european-commission/).

79. Andrew Frye, "Renzi Posts Italy's Biggest Election Victory in 50 Years," Bloomberg, May 26, 2014 (www.bloomberg.com/news/articles/2014-05-25/renzi-set-to-defeat-populist-challenge-in-italy-s-european-vote).

80. International Monetary Fund, "Recovery Strengthens, Remains Uneven," *World Economic Outlook*, April 2014 (www.imf.org/external/pubs/ft/weo/2014/01/).

81. Mario Draghi, "Unemployment in the Euro Area," speech at annual central bank symposium, Jackson Hole, Wyo., August 22, 2014 (www.ecb.europa.eu/press/key/date/2014/html/sp140822.en.html); Mario Draghi, Introductory Statement to the Press Conference, Frankfurt am Main, September 4, 2014 (www.ecb.europa.eu/press/key/date/2014/html/sp140822.en.html).

82. Eric Auchard, "Frankfurt Court Bans Uber Taxi Ser-

vices across Germany," Thomson Reuters, September 2, 2014 (www.reuters.com/article/us-uber-germany-ruling-idUSKBN0 GX0OM20140902).

83. James Politi and Rachel Sanderson, "Italy Calls for New Benchmarks to Measure Reforms," *The Financial Times*, September 7, 2014 (www.ft.com/intl/cms/s/0/dd0a9c00-3691-11e4-95d 3-00144feabdc0.html#axzz3DTCWnlp0).

84. International Monetary Fund, "Global Growth Disappoints, Pace of Recovery Uneven and Country-Specific," *IMF Survey Magazine*, October 7, 2014 (www.imf.org/external/pubs/ ft/survey/so/2014/new100714a.htm).

85. Mario Draghi, "Unemployment in the Euro Area," speech at annual central bank symposium, Jackson Hole, Wyo., August 22, 2014 (www.ecb.europa.eu/press/key/date/2014/html/sp140 822.en.html).

86. International Monetary Fund, "Is It Time for an Infrastructure Push? The Macroeconomic Effects of Public Investment," *World Economic Outlook: Legacies, Clouds, Uncertainties*, October 2014, pp. 75–114 (www.imf.org/external/pubs/ft/weo/ 2014/02/pdf/c3.pdf).

87. International Monetary Fund, "Greece: Ex Post Evaluation of Exceptional Access under the 2010 Stand-By," IMF Country Report No.13/156, June 2013 (www.imf.org/external/ pubs/ft/scr/2013/cr13156.pdf).

88. Reza Moghadam, "Halve Greek Debt and Keep the Eurozone Together," *Financial Times*, January 26, 2015 (www. ft.com/intl/cms/s/0/4cdc1898-9c1c-11e4-a6b6-00144feabdc0. html#axzz3RdIMOknx).

89. Joseph E. Stiglitz, "A Greek Morality Tale," Project Syndicate, February 3, 2015 (www.project-syndicate.org/commentary /greece-eurozone-austerity-reform-by-joseph-e--stiglitz-2015 -02).

90. International Regulatory Framework for Banks (Basel

III), Bank for International Settlements (www.bis.org/bcbs/basel3.htm).

91. Joschka Fischer, "Europe's Migration Paralysis," Project Syndicate, August 24, 2015 (www.project-syndicate.org/commentary/eu-migration-crisis-by-joschka-fischer-2015-08).

92. European Union, EU Law and Publications, "The Schengen Area and Cooperation," last updated on August 3, 2009 (http://eur-lex.europa.eu/legal-content/EN/TXT/?uri=URISERV:l33020).

93. Consolidated Version of the Treaty on the Functioning of the European Union, 2012, O.J./C 326/47-490 (http://eur-lex.europa.eu/legal-content/EN/TXT/PDF/?uri=CELEX:12012E/TXT&from=en).

INDEX